EASTSIDE
SEATTLE WALKS

*20+ routes to explore nature, history, and
public art in Seattle's eastern suburbs*

JANICE M. KING

Published in the United States by Creabunda™ Books, an imprint of WriteSpark Press. Creabunda™ is a trademark of Janice M. King DBA Creabunda (**www.creabunda.com**). All other trademarks and service marks that appear in this book are the property of their respective owners.

First Edition, 2020

Cover and interior design by TeaBerry Creative

PUBLISHER'S CATALOGING-IN-PUBLICATION DATA
provided by Five Rainbows Cataloging Services

Names: King, Janice M., author.

Title: Eastside Seattle walks : 20+ routes to explore nature, history, and public art in Seattle's eastern suburbs / Janice M. King.

Identifiers: ISBN (paperback): 978-0-9766396-2-6 |
ISBN (e-book): 978-0-9766396-3-3

Description: Issaquah, WA : Creabunda Books, 2020. | Includes index.

Subjects: LCSH: Walking—Washington (State)—Seattle—Guidebooks. | Walking—Washington (State)—Guidebooks. | Seattle (Wash.)—Tours. | Seattle Region (Wash.)—Guidebooks. | Travel—Guidebooks. | BISAC: TRAVEL / United States / West / Pacific (AK, CA, HI, OR, WA) | TRAVEL / Special Interest / Hikes & Walks. | TRAVEL / Museums, Tours, Points of Interest.

Classification: LCC F899.S43 K56 2020 (print) |
LCC F899.S43 (ebook) | DDC 917.97/77204—dc23.

*For everyone who enjoys
experiencing and connecting with a place
through walking*

CONTENTS

INTRODUCTION

Welcome to a New Walking Adventure!

The eastern suburbs of Seattle, commonly referred to as the Eastside, offer a wealth of choices for both casual and dedicated walkers. Forested trails, urban sidewalks, country roads, and parkland pathways—all invite exploration.

But with so many possibilities, how can you find the most interesting routes?

That's the purpose of this book: To showcase great walks for discovering and connecting with the many and varied treasures in the cities and towns of the Eastside. Most walks are short, easy or moderately easy, and feature elements that will interest both adults and kids.

For each community, I've chosen a walk that encompasses at least two of these interests: Nature, history, and public art. Some walks include other interests as well, such as gardens, farms, and vintage neighborhoods. And I suggest ideas for additional walks, museums, and other attractions you might enjoy in each area.

How to Use This Guide

Read this section first so you will understand how to use the route descriptions and other information provided in this book when you're considering and following the walk routes described here.

ROUTE DESCRIPTIONS AND FINDING YOUR WAY. Each walk description includes a general overview of the route. Waypoints and street intersections are provided for the starting location and other distinct points along the walk.

When following the routes in this book, stop to read the next direction and orient yourself. You may want to supplement this information with a printed map or a mapping app on a smartphone to confirm your location and provide a visual orientation to the surrounding area.

You'll enjoy the walking experience more if you are prepared and adhere to basic precautions. Always walk with safety in mind, watching and listening for hazards and using crosswalks, pedestrian lights, and flags wherever available.

DIFFICULTY RATING AND SURFACES DESCRIPTION. I have rated all walks in this book as easy or moderately easy, defined as follows:

Easy: Flat or only very slight uphill or downhill grades along some portions of the walk.

Moderately Easy: Mostly flat, but multiple segments involve slight to moderate uphill or downhill grades.

A few walks have segments with steeper uphill or downhill grades; these segments are noted in the route description, along with a bypass if available.

Note: I have not made a judgment about whether any of these routes are considered accessible or ADA compliant, or if they can be navigated by a wheelchair, stroller, or other wheeled device. Read the full route description before starting each walk to determine if it will be suitable for yourself and others in your party.

PARKING AND TRANSIT AVAILABILITY. Each walk includes information on the availability of parking near the starting point. Always check signs for restrictions, time limits, and any required payment. For transit options, the walk description lists the agency that provides nearby service if available, however some walks in this book are not easily accessible by public transit. For details on transit routes, stops, and schedules, check these resources:

King County Metro trip planner: **https://tripplanner.king-county.gov/** (also available as a mobile app)

Snoqualmie Valley Transportation: **http://svtbus.org/**

EXPLORATION IDEAS. The exploration questions and activities are designed to spark curiosity and make the walk more interesting for yourself and your walking companions, especially children.

NATURE INFORMATION. Seattle's Eastside is an area full of natural beauty, with much to enjoy year-round. In winter, we can look for white snow berries and purple beauty berries among the trees and shrubs that remain evergreen. When there's a break in the clouds, we can look both east and west for a glimpse of snow-covered mountains.

In spring, we see the willow branches turning bright green and the shoots of flowering bulbs as we listen to songs that herald arriving birds. On a warm and sunny summer day, we can enjoy the Northwest in its full glory of lush landscapes, stunning views, and perhaps a splash in a local lake. Fall brings its own beauty, with vividly colored leaves glistening after an autumn rain.

Walking in every season offers many discoveries and creates a deeper sense of connection with this very special place. The route descriptions in this book highlight the natural features to enjoy.

ART AND HISTORY RESOURCES. Each route indicates where to look for artworks, although I don't provide details. This is intentional; I want you to look closely at each piece! Look for a sign nearby with the title of the work, name of the artist, and other details. Also, be aware that some artworks may have been removed or new works installed since I wrote the route description.

Be sure to also look for interesting designs and architectural details as you walk: Tree well covers, railings, bike racks, building signs and entrances, bus stop shelters, traffic signal boxes, landscape architecture elements, and designs in sidewalks and planting beds. Read the nameplates on park benches, bricks, and donor walls; you may find some interesting messages that way! Tracking your discoveries can be a fun activity to do with kids.

Keep an eye out for signs or plaques that present information and pictures about the history of an area, building, or site. Many Eastside communities have a local heritage society and there are several small history museums in the area; these resources are listed for the individual walks.

Additionally, you may want to download a tag reader app and the STQRY app (**https://www.stqry.com/**) on your smartphone for scanning the special barcodes on signs where available; these codes will link to a webpage with more information. And be sure to explore the additional resources listed on the companion website for this book: **www.eastsideseattlewalks.com**

Getting the Most from Every Walk

I believe walking, without electronic distractions and with an openness to discovery, is a great way to get a sense of connection and belonging to a place. If you're walking with a companion, you can enjoy joint discoveries and the differences in what catches each other's eye. And if walking with children, you'll have the enjoyment of seeing the world as a fun playground again.

So get out by choosing a walk from this book, whether close to home or in an area you haven't yet explored. Take the time to really see and listen to the nature around you, to really look at the artwork, and to read history signs and imagine that place in times past. You'll likely see familiar surroundings in a whole new way.

Janice King

NORTHERN WALKS

→ BOTHELL
→ KENMORE
→ KIRKLAND
→ REDMOND
→ WOODINVILLE

Built along the lake shore or riverbank, the northern communities still offer many views into their historic and natural past, enhanced by the art of today.

Stormwater drainage areas, such as this one in Bothell, often contain a variety of Northwest native plants.

BOTHELL: DOWNTOWN

URBAN VILLAGE THROUGH TIME

A loop route from the natural riverfront through a booming business and residential district, with plenty of history and art along the way.

LENGTH: About 1.5 miles

DIFFICULTY RATING: Moderately Easy

SURFACES: Sidewalks and paved trails

STARTING POINT: Bothell Landing Park, corner of Bothell Way NE and 98th Ave. NE.

PARKING: Street parking at Bothell Landing Park, on Main St., and on side streets

PUBLIC TRANSIT: King County Metro

KIDS WILL ENJOY: Bothell Landing Park offers a playground, river access, and the buildings of the Bothell Historical Museum, where interesting displays and volunteer docents explain local life in a way that is entertaining for adults and kids.

SERVICES ALONG ROUTE OR NEARBY: Restrooms located at Bothell Landing Park, Library, and City Hall. Restaurants, gas, and retail along Main St., Bothell Way NE, and side streets.

Route Description

BOTHELL LANDING PARK This walk starts at the cluster of historic buildings that make up the Bothell Historical Museum. Explore the Victorian home, log cabin, and schoolhouse buildings if open.

Facing south, look for the arched bridge across the river to the left. Walk to the bridge for a view of the Sammamish River where, in the late summer and fall, you may see salmon swimming upstream to spawn. On the opposite side of the bridge is the Sammamish River Trail, which you can follow to the west to reach Seattle or to the east to reach Woodinville.

To continue this walk, turn around and return to the historic buildings area, noticing the river-themed bicycle rack near the log cabin and the picnic tables behind with a river view.

Walk west around the play area and follow the trail to the metal bridge over Horse Creek. A boat launch area provides direct river access; a picnic area is also located here.

BOTHELL WAY NE AND 98TH AVE. NE TO NE 183RD ST.
Return to the play area and follow the path on the west side
to reach the park access road. Turn left and follow the sidewalk to the intersection of Bothell Way NE and 98th Ave. NE.
Cross Bothell Way to view the public art installation at the
northwest corner.

Walk north on 98th Ave. NE to the Bothell Library at NE 183rd
St. An information sign explains the rain gardens outside;
also look for several book-themed bronze sculptures near the
library entrance.

*Look closely and you'll see a companion bear
through this window at the Bothell Library.*

NE 183RD ST. TO BOTHELL WAY NE Cross 98th Ave. NE at the crosswalk on the north side of NE 183rd St. Notice the sign with the historic street name. Continue east, crossing to the east side of Bothell Way NE, then turn right/south and cross NE 183rd St.

BOTHELL WAY AND MAIN ST. TO 102ND AVE. NE Go one block south to Main St. and turn left/east. On the northwest corner of Main and 101st Ave. NE look at the mural of Bothell history painted on the building side. As you continue walking east, look for historical photos on the side of utility boxes along the sidewalk and painted cutouts of business people from the town's history.

Turn left/north on 102nd Ave. NE, and notice the arched shape of the church building at the southeast corner of 102nd Ave. NE and NE 183rd St., reflecting the community's Scandinavian heritage.

102ND AVE. NE TO NE 183RD ST. TO BOTHELL CITY HALL Walk west on NE 183rd St. to Bothell City Hall. An art gallery inside is open during business hours. Outside, look for bronze otter sculptures in the fountain area. Also look southeast to see another history mural on the back of one of the Main St. buildings.

BOTHELL CITY HALL TO BOTHELL WAY NE Walk west on NE 183rd St. to Bothell Way NE, then turn left/south and walk two blocks to return to Bothell Landing Park.

The schoolhouse and two other relocated buildings of the Bothell History Museum will give you an engaging look into the town's early development.

Exploration Ideas

- Along Main St., make a treasure hunt of looking for the history signs, murals, cutout figures, and photos on utility boxes.
- The public art installation at Bothell Way NE and 98th Ave. NE. contains multiple elements, with common themes. Which ones do you see? How do they relate to local nature?
- At the library, did you find the inside and outside bear sculptures?
- Did you notice the decorative metal fences and tree well covers around the street trees?

Nearby Walks and Points of Interest

UW Bothell/Cascadia College Campus walk (see next walk)

The "Town to Gown Loop Walk," developed by the University of Washington, provides directions to walk from downtown Bothell to the UW campus with information on history signs and landmarks along the way. Map available at: **https://www.uwb.edu/getattachment/about/around-bothell/TownGown2pager-(1).pdf**

Check for Updated Information

City of Bothell: **http://www.ci.bothell.wa.us/**
Bothell Historical Museum:
http://www.bothellhistoricalmuseum.org/
Bothell Library: **http://kcls.org/locations/1493/**
University of Washington Bothell: **www.uwb.edu**

The garden area next to the UW Bothell Truly House offers a flower-filled oasis.

BOTHELL: UW BOTHELL/CASCADIA COLLEGE CAMPUS

ART, FARMHOUSES & CROWS

Walk through campus to discover imaginative art, glimpses of farm life, and a restored wetland.

LENGTH: About 1.5 miles

DIFFICULTY RATING: Moderate; some significant uphill and downhill segments

SURFACES: Sidewalks, paved and dirt trails

STARTING POINT: North campus parking garage

PARKING: All campus parking requires payment. In the north garage, look for the payment kiosk at the south end, next to the elevator.

PUBLIC TRANSIT: King County Metro, Community Transit

KIDS WILL ENJOY: Some of the outdoor artworks, the historic homes, and the campus vegetable garden will be engaging for imaginative minds. Older children may enjoy experiencing the mass arrival of crows during roosting season.

SERVICES ALONG ROUTE OR NEARBY: Restrooms, restaurants, and retail located in campus buildings during weekday open hours. Restaurants and retail approximately two blocks north of campus; gas in downtown Bothell.

NOTE: Campus buildings may not be open on weekends or during college vacations; check the websites listed below for information on open hours and public access before visiting. Also, the campus is a major, seasonal roosting site for crows and ravens, which arrive in tremendous numbers around sunset. Although some people will enjoy seeing this sight, it may be overwhelming for others. The roosting activity also creates special considerations for accessing the campus wetlands; see the note for that section of the walk.

Route Description

NORTH PARKING GARAGE As you leave the south end of the garage, look for a metal sculpture facing the soccer field. Be sure to read the text and look at different images on the individual panels.

CAMPUS WAY NE Cross the main campus drive and follow the sidewalk north alongside the Cascadia College building, then turn left/west at the first set of bus shelters. Walk to the second bus shelter and notice the four stone and steel benches.

Walk back to the sidewalk between shelters and turn right/south and follow the sidewalk between buildings. A small art gallery is in Mobius Hall, the first building on the right/west; visit during the building's open hours.

In the central plaza area between buildings, notice the vibrant colors of the painted peace poles. Continuing south, look for the grouping of carved wood sculptures; a rough dirt path leads uphill for a close-up view.

Note: This section of the walk involves dirt trails and steep uphill and downhill segments. For an alternate route, return to your car then drive to the surface parking area just south of the Truly Farmhouse.

TRULY FARMHOUSE Follow the path uphill and to the left/south to reach the Truly Farmhouse, an historic craftsman style bungalow built in 1888. The building is not open to the public, but the rose garden and picnic table on the north side make a good resting spot. A sign on the west side of this area explains the farming history of this property.

Walk to the south side of the farmhouse then along the driveway to the stairs at the north side of Discovery Hall. Walk down the stairs to return to the main campus walkway, noticing the native planting beds and the rain steps between the stairs and Discovery Hall.

At the large plaza, turn left to enter the UW Bothell Library courtyard. Look for the paving stones with letters and numbers and the bicycle racks with bronze sculptures on top. If the library is open, go inside to view an extensive collection of Northwest native artworks on walls and in display cases. The library also contains several other artworks and historical photos of the property when it was the Truly ranch. Download a guide to the art in this building from the link below.

This group of life-size sculptures stands in a forested area on the UW Bothell campus.

Exit the library and turn right/south to walk on the main campus walkway until you reach the street. Turn left/east onto the sidewalk on NE 180th St. and walk downhill to the intersection with Campus Way NE (very steep).

The relocated Chase house brings a sense of 19th-century Bothell history to a 20th-century college campus.

NE 180TH ST. AND CAMPUS WAY NE Cross to the east side of the main campus drive, then follow the sidewalk south to see the historic Chase house, relocated to this site (not open to the public). A small garden and orchard area give the feel of a homestead, with benches and a picnic table for a break.

The crosswalk leading east from the Chase house takes you to the nature trail. Turn left/north onto the main trail, which is paved and flat although the access trail has a slight downhill. As you begin your walk on this trail, notice how what was once farmland is now a diverse wetland. Look for information signs along the trail with information about this restored ecosystem.

Note: Between the baseball and soccer fields you will notice a trail leading to the right for a boardwalk that takes you deeper into the wetland and a view of the restored route of North Creek. However, the boardwalk is often covered with waste from the thousands of crows and ravens that roost in this area at night. This waste can create a strong and unpleasant smell and make the walking surface of the trail and boardwalk very slippery. If you want to avoid walking on this side trail, continue on the main trail.

SOCCER FIELD At the north side of the soccer field, look for a concrete and stone seating area that honors military service; be sure to read the text that encircles the center stone.

To return to the parking garage, take the path along the north side of the soccer field, enjoying the student garden area on the right. Turn right at the sidewalk to follow the ramp uphill to reach the garage or the bus shelter at the north end of campus.

Exploration Ideas

- *What do the large wood sculptures on the hill and the sculptures in the library courtyard make you think about?*
- *What evidence of the roosting site for crows and ravens did you find?*
- *What do you think this area looked like when it was a farm?*

Nearby Walks and Points of Interest

Bothell: Downtown Walk (see previous walk)

The "Town to Gown Loop Walk," provides directions to walk from downtown Bothell to the UW Bothell/Cascadia campus with information on history signs and landmarks along the way. Map available at: **https://www.uwb.edu/getattachment/ about/around-bothell/TownGown2pager-(1).pdf**

Check for Updated Information

University of Washington Bothell General information: **https://www.uwb.edu** Crow roosting activity: **https://www.uwb.edu/visitors/crows** Library art collection: **https://cdm16786.contentdm.oclc. org/digital/collection/p16786coll14** and **http://libguides. uwb.edu/nativeart** Cascadia College General information: **http://www.cascadia.edu** Mobius Hall art gallery: **http://www.cascadia.edu/discover/ visitors/gallery.aspx**

Kenmore's Log Boom Park offers a guide to local history along the main walking path.

KENMORE

A waterfront trail and park give a view of local history and the industrial side of Lake Washington.

LENGTH: About .25 miles

DIFFICULTY RATING: Easy

SURFACES: Sidewalks and paved pier.

STARTING POINT: Log Boom Park, 17415 61st Ave. NE, Kenmore, WA 98028

PARKING: Parking lot at the park

PUBLIC TRANSIT: None nearby

KIDS WILL ENJOY: Playground area; watching the ducks or fishing from the pier.

SERVICES ALONG ROUTE OR NEARBY: Restrooms located at the park. Restaurants, gas, and retail along NE Bothell Way.

Route Description

· ·

LOG BOOM PARK ENTRANCE Look for the entrance sign to the history path at the southeast corner of the parking lot. Learn about local history from the multiple signs along this path as it leads toward Lake Washington. Enjoy the nature provided by the grassy area and native plantings along the path until you reach the pier area. Benches and picnic tables are located near the pier entrance.

PIER Walk onto the paved pier for a view back to the nature area and south down Lake Washington. Look for water birds as well as floatplane landings and takeoffs. Retrace your route to return to the parking lot, but look for another paved path at the west end of the lot to continue this walk.

PLAYGROUND AREA Walk west past the playground to view a ceramic art panel with a heron design, installed on the outside of the restroom building. Continue walking west to reach a small grass and sandy beach area for a quieter view of the lake. To finish this walk, retrace your route east, walking past the playground to the parking lot.

Exploration Ideas

- *What did you learn about local history by reading the signs along the trail?*

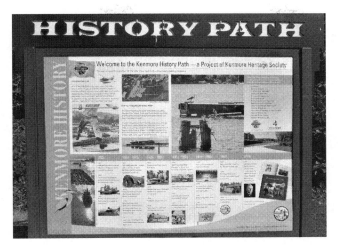

*Detailed signs along the Log Boom Park path focus
on the many dimensions of Kenmore history*

Nearby Walks and Points of Interest

Public artworks are located at the Kenmore Library (6531 NE
181st St.) and Kenmore City Hall (18120 68th Ave. NE), which
also has a public art gallery.

The Burke Gilman Trail can be accessed on the north side of
the park and provides a paved pathway that extends east past
industrial Kenmore.

Check for Updated Information

City of Kenmore: **www.kenmorewa.gov**
Kenmore Heritage Society: **http://kenmoreheritag-
esociety.com/**
Kenmore Library: **https://kcls.org/locations/1519/**

KIRKLAND ARTS CENTER
Art School & Gallery

The Kirkland Arts Center offers an art gallery and classes in the historic Peter Kirk building.

KIRKLAND

This art-filled town offers open vistas of water and many reminders of history.

LENGTH: About 1.75 miles (full route), less than 1 mile for downtown portion

DIFFICULTY RATING: Moderately easy. Some parts of the route involve rough and narrow sidewalks; the walk from Marina Park to Kirkland Arts Center and return involves steep uphill and downhill blocks.

SURFACES: Sidewalks and gravel paths

STARTING POINT: Kirkland Library, 308 Kirkland Ave., Kirkland, WA 98033

PARKING: Public parking garage underneath the library; don't use the spots marked for library patrons. Street parking and paid parking lots throughout the downtown area.

PUBLIC TRANSIT: King County Metro

Kirkland is known for its many panoramic views of Lake Washington.

KIDS WILL ENJOY: Beach area with lake access at Marina Park and large grassy area at Heritage Park; whimsical sculptures throughout downtown; playground at Peter Kirk Park next to library.

SERVICES ALONG ROUTE OR NEARBY: Restrooms in library and Marina Park. Restaurants and retail throughout the downtown area; gas on Central Way and NE 85th St. east of I-405.

Route Description

KIRKLAND LIBRARY Begin this walk at the library entrance, viewing the carousel sculpture on the lawn area in front and the painted tiles attached to the building exterior. Multiple artworks are installed inside the library; restrooms also located here.

KIRKLAND AVE. TO LAKE ST. From the library, cross to the planted area at the southwest corner of Kirkland Ave. and 3rd St./State St. to view the large bronze sculpture of two bears. Walk west along the south side of Kirkland Ave., noticing the heritage sign for the building that previously occupied this corner.

At the southwest corner of Main St. and Kirkland Ave., look for a pole with metal birdhouses in the planting area. On the northeast corner, look for the sculpture of a seated woman enjoying the sun. Continue west and at the southeast corner of Lake St. and Kirkland Ave., see the stone sculpture fountain installation and the traffic signal box wrapped with historical photos of this intersection and the lakeside ferry dock. As you look to the west side of Lake St., the smaller buildings here are reminders of Kirkland's small-town past.

LAKE ST. TO MARINA PARK Cross Lake St. and continue west on Kirkland Ave. to reach Marina Park. Walk onto the dock for a close-up view of Lake Washington and visiting boats. Also notice the sailor homecoming sculpture at the dock entrance, the decorative railing on top of the concrete utility building, the word design embedded in the concrete next to the park restrooms, and a sculptural fountain near the beach area. Picnic tables and benches offer a good spot to enjoy the lake view.

Follow the main path through the park as it curves northwest around the lake toward the pavilion. Look for the fountain and jumping children sculpture at the top of the grassy area nearby.

From the pavilion benches, enjoy another view of the lake and the Seattle shoreline.

MARINA PARK TO MARKET ST./HERITAGE PARK Exit the pavilion and follow the sidewalk north/uphill. Cross Lake Ave. West and view the historic Heritage Hall, which was moved to this site after a City Hall expansion. A nearby sign tells the story of this building. The Kirkland Heritage Society maintains offices here; check their website or call for open hours.

Return to the main sidewalk and walk north on the west side of Market St. A garden area behind Heritage Hall makes a pleasant resting stop if it is not in use for a private event. *Important Note:* From this point, sidewalks become rough and the walk involves several steep uphill and downhill blocks. To avoid this section, cross to the northeast corner of Market St. and Central Way, walk east to the intersection with Lake St., then follow the route from that point.

At the corner of Waverly Way and Market St. is Heritage Park, with a large grassy area that provides more lake views. Also here are the ivy-covered remains of the entryway to Kirkland Junior High School, which stood on this site for many years after its construction in 1932.

MARKET ST. TO 7TH AVE. Return to Market St. and turn left/ north for three blocks. Notice the remaining vintage cottage and craftsman style homes. When you reach 7th Ave., look for the historic brick buildings around this intersection. A sign on the modern building at the southwest corner explains the history of this area for Kirkland's founding and development.

Cross to the southeast corner of Market St. and 7th Ave. to visit the gallery and classrooms of the Kirkland Arts Center if open; also read the history sign at the building's entrance.

MARKET ST. TO 6TH AVE. AND 1ST ST. Walk south on the east side of Market St., then turn left on 6th Ave. and walk one block east to 1st St. and turn right to see more historic homes and the Kirkland Women's Club building, constructed in 1924.

1ST ST. OR MARKET ST. TO CENTRAL WAY Walk south down a steep hill on 1st St. to Central Way; for a less steep route, turn right at 4th Ave. and return to Market St.

CENTRAL WAY TO LAKE ST. Turn left/east at Central Way and walk to the intersection of Lake St. At the northwest corner, look for the cow and coyote sculpture, often decorated for various celebrations. Cross to the southwest corner to see the bronze rabbits and notice the glass mosaic elements embedded in the sidewalk, then cross to the southeast corner to view the history photos on the traffic signal box.

LAKE ST. TO PARK LANE TO 3RD ST. Walk one block south to Park Lane, then turn left onto the south sidewalk. Walk east on Park Lane, noticing the sculptures located on both sidewalks. *Caution:* Park Lane is NOT a pedestrian-only street; watch and listen for cars.

Cross Main St. and continue east on Park Lane to the intersection with 3rd St. On the northwest corner, look for artwork installed on two sides of the water pump station building. Cross 3rd St. at the pedestrian intersection and notice the granite installation on the stairs leading to the parking garage and library.

Public art can be found in surprising places, such as this utility station in downtown Kirkland.

Exploration Ideas

- How many animal and people sculptures did you see on the walk?

- What did you learn about local Kirkland history? How does that change how you see the town now?

- What are all the ways you can enjoy nature at the lake?

Nearby Walks and Points of Interest

The Cross Kirkland Corridor is a former railroad route that has been converted to a walking and bicycling trail; nearest access from downtown is at 7th Ave. and 112th Ave. NE.

Check for updated info:

City of Kirkland: **https://www.Kirklandwa.gov/home.htm**
Cross Kirkland Corridor: **https://www.kirklandwa.gov/ Residents/Community/Cross_Kirkland_Corridor.htm**
Kirkland public art: **http://www.exploreKirkland.com/Arts/ Public_Art.htm**
Kirkland Library: **http://kcls.org/locations/1518/**
Kirkland Arts Center: **http://www.kirklandartscenter.org/**
Kirkland Heritage Society: **http://Kirklandheritage.org/**

Downtown Park, the newest in Redmond,
offers a fun selfie spot on the artfully designed stage.

REDMOND WALK #1: DOWNTOWN SOUTH

HISTORIC RURAL TOWN TO VIBRANT URBAN CENTER

*In a downtown with much new development,
a loop walk explores pockets of history,
parks, the riverside, and public art.*

LENGTH: About 1.7 miles

DIFFICULTY RATING: Easy

SURFACES: Paved pathways and sidewalks; grass areas in Downtown Park and Dudley Carter Park

STARTING POINT: Bear Creek Parkway and 161st Ave. NE, Redmond, WA 98052

PARKING: Street parking on Bear Creek Parkway or pay parking lot at corner of Bear Creek Parkway and Leary Way

PUBLIC TRANSIT: King County Metro

KIDS WILL ENJOY: Large lawn and water play area at Redmond Downtown Park; seeing birds and salmon swimming upstream in the Sammamish River.

*The Sammamish River runs through Redmond,
offering a natural respite in a busy city.*

SERVICES ALONG ROUTE OR NEARBY: Restrooms located at Redmond Downtown Park and in Redmond Town Center shopping area. Restaurants, gas, and retail located throughout the downtown area.

Route Description

BEAR CREEK PARKWAY AND 161ST AVE. NE/DOWNTOWN REDMOND CONNECTOR Starting at the northeast corner, enter the Downtown Redmond Connector, a set of pathways and park areas that extends along the route of an old railroad line. You'll see a tribute to this history as you follow the path east, where it curves left then reaches a public artwork made in part from historic Redmond railroad signals. Also look for pieces of railroad track embedded in the path.

Continue east on the main pathway for one block. At the parking lot, notice the vibrant blue and yellow painted design on the pavement, another public artwork, designed to reflect the rings of local trees.

LEARY WAY Use the crosswalk at the east end of the parking lot/Leary Way (no street sign) to continue east on the pathway, noticing the change in buildings that indicate how Redmond is transitioning from the small town of its history to an urban center of today.

DOWNTOWN REDMOND CONNECTOR Continue east at the crosswalk on 164th Ave. NE and walk one block to see the third public art piece on this pathway, a large metal sculpture that acknowledges glacial activity in the area.

Retrace your steps along the pathway to return to Leary Way for the first history stop, the Justice White House, once a railroad hotel and now a private office building. Use the crosswalk at NE 76th St. for a close-up look. For a detailed description of the site and other historic buildings in the downtown area, load the Redmond Historical Society's *Steps in Time* app on your smartphone.

LEARY WAY TO REDMOND WAY Return to Leary Way and walk north on the east sidewalk, noticing the red brick architecture of the historic buildings. Cross at Cleveland St. and Redmond Way to continue north; more vintage buildings on these blocks will give you a sense of the historic downtown.

After two blocks, cross to the west side of the street, then walk south to return to the southwest corner of Redmond Way and Leary Way. A kiosk here presents information on the buildings you've seen and many historic photos. Be sure to look at both sides of the kiosk, at the clock tower above, and at the foliage design of the benches in this area.

REDMOND WAY TO REDMOND DOWNTOWN PARK Walk west on Redmond Way one block to Redmond Downtown Park. Walk on the sidewalk to the east side of the park; at the southeast corner, notice the stone house, an historic landmark. Also look up to see the two sets of lights strung across the crosswalk as a public art installation over Cleveland St. Take a few minutes to explore the park; seating areas with tables, a water play area, and restrooms located here.

REDMOND DOWNTOWN PARK TO 161ST AVE. NE AND BEAR CREEK PARKWAY NE. Leave the park heading west and cross to the southwest corner of 161st Ave. NE and Cleveland St. Walk south on 161st Ave. NE and cross Bear Creek Parkway. Follow the pathway as it curves right on the east side of the apartment buildings and offers views into a natural forest area, which also serves as a nesting site for herons.

BEAR CREEK PARKWAY TO DUDLEY CARTER PARK When the pathway reaches Leary Way, turn right and cross 159th Pl. NE. On the northwest corner is Dudley Carter Park, the home site of a noted local carver of native art. Look at the carvings on the hand-built woodworking shop and the carved tree at the west side of the property, next to the Sammamish River Trail.

Walk onto the river trail, facing the bridge. You'll see a connection go under the bridge for a close-up view of the river or walk onto the pedestrian bridge for a good look down, especially in the fall when salmon are swimming upstream. Retrace your steps on the forest trail to return to Bear Creek Parkway.

Exploration Ideas

- *In Downtown Park, look for the structure that is designed as a performance stage, but is also an artwork. It has a mirrored ceiling that makes for a fun selfie photo, especially if you and your walking companions lie on the stage floor.*

- *Do you know another word for the heron nesting area? Answer: Rookery.*

- *Late August to mid-October is prime time to look for salmon swimming upstream at the Sammamish River Bridge. Also look for great blue herons, ducks, and other birds along the riverbank.*

Nearby Walks and Points of Interest

. . . .

The Redmond Farmers Market is located behind the Justice White House building on Saturdays during the season; check **http://redmondsaturdaymarket.org/**.

From the Sammamish River Trail bridge, you can connect to the other Redmond walks:

Turn north to combine this walk with Redmond Walk #2: Downtown North (see next walk). Start with the instructions for walking north from Dudley Carter Park. When you reach the Redmond Library, read the instructions at the beginning of Redmond Walk #2 for a return route to this point.

Turn south to combine this walk with Redmond Walk #3: Marymoor Park (see walk later in this section). Start with the instructions for walking south from Dudley Carter Park, then reverse the route to return.

Check for Updated Information

City of Redmond: **http://www.redmond.gov/**

Redmond public art collection information:
http://www.redmond.gov/publicart

Redmond Historical Society and link to the Steps in
Time app: **http://www.redmondhistoricalsociety.org/
RHS/index.php**

Redmond has made a park of the former home and workshop site of woodcarver Dudley Carter, whose Northwest native-influenced works can be seen around the city.

REDMOND WALK #2: DOWNTOWN NORTH

ART & NATURE ON A RIVERSIDE STROLL

See birds, salmon, native plants, and numerous artworks on this round-trip walk along a riverside trail and the City Hall campus.

LENGTH: About 2 miles

DIFFICULTY RATING: Easy

SURFACES: Sidewalks and paved and gravel pathways; grass areas in Dudley Carter Park

STARTING POINT: Redmond Library, 15990 NE 85th St., Redmond, WA 98052

PARKING: Street parking; do not park in the lots for the Redmond Library or Redmond City Hall

PUBLIC TRANSIT: King County Metro

KIDS WILL ENJOY: Large lawn areas at Dudley Carter Park, Luke McRedmond Landing, and Redmond City Hall. Seeing birds and salmon swimming upstream in the Sammamish River.

SERVICES ALONG ROUTE OR NEARBY: Restrooms located at Redmond Library and Redmond City Hall. Restaurants, gas, and retail located throughout the downtown area.

Route Description

REDMOND LIBRARY Start at the library's west entrance, where you are welcomed by a stone sculpture of ravens. To the left of the book return, look for the carved wood sculpture by local artist Dudley Carter, the first of several you'll see on this walk. Go inside the library entrance hall to see a rotating exhibit of artworks on one wall and three Dudley Carter sculptures on the other. Other art pieces are on display inside the main library space.

From the east library door, turn left and walk on the sidewalk to the north side of the building. Explore the sculpture garden in this area.

REDMOND DISTRICT COURT TO PARKING GARAGE From the sculpture garden, follow the sidewalk west, then turn right/ north on the sidewalk in front of the Redmond District Court building. Continue on the sidewalk as it curves right, then cross the roadway and follow the sidewalk north to reach the parking garage. Can you see the artistic installation on the side of this structure?

*Look for these metal boats, a public art installation
on the Redmond municipal parking garage.*

POLICE BUILDING TO SENIOR CENTER From the parking garage, cross the entrance road to the south side and notice the first of four tile panels installed on the side of the police building complex. Continue right/west on the sidewalk toward the senior center to see the remaining panels. Follow the sidewalk to the open park area; notice the metal sculpture in front of a large oak tree.

SAMMAMISH RIVER TRAIL Turn right/west and walk toward the river trail, noticing the two laser-cut metal sculptures to your left and one on the right. Picnic tables in this area.

Turn left/south onto the river trail, looking and listening for bicycles before you enter. Notice the native plants and views of the river on the right; benches and nature information signs are at several locations along the trail. As you pass Redmond City Hall, notice the large stone sculpture on the lawn and the bronze sculpture of the seated woman.

Walk under the bridge and notice the sandy area to the right that provides direct river access. After the bridge, you'll see a garden area on the left to explore on the return walk.

LUKE MCREDMOND LANDING Continue on the trail, walking under an old railroad bridge and another street bridge. Just past the street bridge, look left for another Dudley Carter sculpture. Then look right for a paved path that slopes downward, with a bronze sculpture of beavers and river access.

Return to the main pathway and turn right/south. Picnic tables and benches are in the park here. As you continue walking, enjoy the more open view of the river on this part of the trail.

DUDLEY CARTER PARK Continue until you reach the next park, previously the home site of a noted local carver of native art. Look at the carvings on the hand-built woodworking studio (called the Haida House) and the carved tree at the west side of the property.

Return to the river trail, facing the bridge. Walk to the connection under the bridge for a close-up view of the river or walk onto the pedestrian bridge for a good look down, especially in the fall when salmon are swimming upstream.

To return to the starting point for this walk at the Redmond Library, retrace your steps walking north on the Sammamish River Trail. When you reach the garden area, explore the small gravel paths and read the plant identification signs; benches located in this area.

After walking under the NE 85th St. bridge, take an immediate right/east onto the path and sidewalk on the south side of Redmond City Hall. At the east side of City Hall, turn left to the main entrance area and look at the light sculpture and water feature. Notice how the mirror panels create new images as you walk around and view the sculpture from different angles.

From here, return to your car or use the sidewalk on NE 85th St. to return to the Redmond Library.

Exploration Ideas

- *Did you see the boat design in the art installation on the side of the parking garage?*
- *Can you imagine what the river would have been like when steamships offered the best way to travel?*
- *What does the title of an artwork make you think or feel about it? Have you seen similar artworks on other walks?*
- *Look for herons along the river, often standing so still they seem to be a sculpture instead of a living bird!*

Nearby Walks and Points of Interest

From the Sammamish River Trail bridge, you can connect to the other Redmond walks:

Turn east to combine this walk with Redmond Walk #1: Downtown South (see previous walk). Start with the instructions for the return from Dudley Carter Park.

Turn south to combine this walk with Redmond Walk #3 to Marymoor Park (see next walk).

Check for Updated Info

City of Redmond: **http://www.redmond.gov/244/walking**
Redmond public art walking map: **http://www.redmond.gov/
documentcenter/view/1409**
Redmond Library: **http://kcls.org/locations/1533/**
Redmond Historical Society and link to the Steps in
Time app: **http://www.redmondhistoricalsociety.org/
RHS/index.php**

The historic windmill in Redmond's Marymoor Park was built when this area was a working farm.

REDMOND WALK #3: MARYMOOR PARK

TREASURES AMONG THE BALLFIELDS

Explore historic farm buildings and unexpected artworks in a large and popular park.

LENGTH: About 1 mile

DIFFICULTY RATING: Easy

SURFACES: Paved and dirt pathways, some narrow or rough; grass areas around Clise Mansion

STARTING POINT: Marymoor Park parking lot for Willowmoor Farm/Clise Mansion, near west park entrance, 6046 West Lake Sammamish Pkwy NE, Redmond, WA 98052

PARKING: All park lots require payment of a daily fee; see posted signs and payment kiosks for rates and rules

PUBLIC TRANSIT: King County Metro

KIDS WILL ENJOY: Large lawn areas, windmill at Clise Mansion, playground areas east of the Clise Mansion and near the softball fields.

SERVICES ALONG ROUTE OR NEARBY: Restrooms located at east playground area and near softball fields. Restaurants, gas, and retail located throughout downtown Redmond.

Route Description

WILLOWMOOR FARM PARKING LOT Begin at the north side of the parking lot, where you'll see the carved totem pole by Redmond artist Dudley Carter; you can see other works by this artist on Redmond Walks #1 and #2. Be sure to walk around all sides of the pole to see all of the carvings.

Walk south through the parking lot to the small house that is now the park office. You'll find helpful park maps and brochures on display by the front door (stairs-only access).

Walk west and follow the narrow paved sidewalk to reach the formal front gates of the historic Clise Mansion.

CLISE MANSION AREA Follow the paved path to the right/west toward the historic shingled windmill. Benches and picnic tables located throughout this grassy area. A fenced area just north of the windmill provides a winter view of the Sammamish River. Return to the main path and turn right/southwest, noticing the variety of trees and shrubs planted in this area.

Stay on the main path as it turns left/east and enjoy the views of the mansion grounds. At the three-way split of the trail, walk left/north toward the Clise Mansion (not open to the public). Walk around the building to see the architecture details such as the sunroom on the south side, the leaded glass windows on the north side, and the history sign on the west side. To the east of the mansion you'll find more interesting trees and a playground area with restrooms.

WILLOWMOOR FARM PARKING LOT Walk to the parking lot entrance and cross the main park drive at the stop sign. *Important Note:* No crosswalk here. Walk straight through Parking Lot K to the small fenced area behind the information kiosk. Here you'll find a public artwork in the form of a mandala-shaped reflexology path with a stone bird bath in the center and instructions in multiple languages. Restrooms in this area.

From here, retrace your steps through Parking Lot K to return to the Willowmoor Farm parking lot.

Exploration Ideas

- *Can you imagine this area when it was a farm? When it was a hunting and fishing campsite for native people?*

Nearby Walks and Points of Interest

This walk connects with Redmond Walks #1 and #2 at Dudley Carter Park (see walk information earlier in this section). From Parking Lot K, walk west approximately one-quarter mile on the paved path along the south side of the ball fields to reach the Sammamish River Trail, crossing the bridge over the river. Turn right/north on the trail and walk approximate 1 mile to reach Dudley Carter Park.

Within Marymoor Park, the Eastside Audubon chapter maintains a birdwatching loop trail, accessed from Parking Lot G.

Check for Updated Info

Marymoor Park: **https://www.kingcounty.gov/services/ parks-recreation/parks/parks-and-natural-lands/popu- lar-parks/marymoor.aspx**
Eastside Audubon Society: **https://www.eastside- audubon.org/**

*The Marymoor Park playground, with its artistic play structures,
can be a fun way to encourage kids to look for art.*

*Look for history signs as you walk through the archway
at Woodinville's Wilmot Gateway Park.*

WOODINVILLE

FRESH FINDS IN WINE COUNTRY

Known for its many local wineries, Woodinville is also rich in history, art, and agriculture.

LENGTH: About 1.25 miles

DIFFICULTY RATING: Easy

SURFACES: Sidewalks and paved paths

STARTING POINT: Wilmot Gateway Park, 17301 131st Ave. NE, Woodinville, WA 98072

PARKING: Parking lot at Wilmot Gateway Park or at the ballfields to the east

PUBLIC TRANSIT: King County Metro

KIDS WILL ENJOY: Lawn areas at the parks, playground at Wilmot Gateway Park, and looking at imaginative artworks

SERVICES ALONG ROUTE OR NEARBY: Restrooms located at the north end of the arbor in Wilmot Gateway Park. Restaurants, gas, and retail along NE 175th St.

Route Description

. . . .

WILMOT GATEWAY PARK TO WOODIN CREEK PARK This walk starts at the south end of the arbor in Wilmot Gateway Park. Walk through the arbor and notice the tiles with historic images at one of the parking lot entrances. Facing the lawn area, turn right on the paved path and look for an information sign about local nature, the metal sculpture just north of the playground area, and the painted peace pole behind the restroom building.

Walk to the paved Sammamish River Trail pathway, looking and listening carefully for oncoming bicyclists. Walk north to see the painted mural next to the path as it passes under the NE. 175th St. bridge.

Staying on the trail, turn south and look for a sign about historic transportation uses for the river. Walk approximately .1 mile to the first path on the left and enter Woodin Creek Park (no sign; look for the picnic shelter and tennis court to confirm you're on the correct trail). Walk north through the park, noticing the poles with bat boxes on your right and a large metal sculpture near the basketball court.

WOODIN CREEK PARK TO NE 171ST ST. AND 135TH AVE. NE
Exit the park at the entrance on NE 171st St. and turn right/east along the south sidewalk. Walk to the second roundabout to see a large steel sculpture and farmland to the south. Cross to the north sidewalk to see a creekside restoration area with native plants. Staying on the north sidewalk, retrace your path northwest until you reach 133rd Ave. NE.

135TH AVE. NE TO 133RD AVE. NE TO NE 175TH ST. Turn right/north on 133rd Ave. NE, noticing the progression from new to old Woodinville as you pass new apartments and mixed-use buildings, a 1970s-era strip mall, and the Woodinville High School building from 1938.

Important Note: As of late 2019, the high school area was under construction and some sidewalks and access points may be closed. Look for detour signs or follow the instructions below from Woodinville City Hall.

Walk in front of the old high school and look for the original cemetery opposite, on the northwest corner of NE 175th St. and 133rd Ave NE. If you want a closer view of the many pioneer graves located here, walk one block to 131st Ave. NE where you can use the crosswalk at the stoplight.

NE 175TH ST. TO CITY HALL To continue from the west side of the old school, turn south along the driveway, then a slight right turn and down a paved ramp to the path along the ballfields. Take a close look at the mural painted on the north and west sides of the recreation building, featuring scenes and symbols of Woodinville.

Continue on the path past the ballfields until you reach the west side of City Hall. Notice the metal sculpture in the shape of a trumpet flower on the lawn and the artistic bike rack near the building entrance.

Even ordinary objects can have an artistic flair, such as this bicycle rack at Woodinville City Hall.

CITY HALL TO WILMOT GATEWAY PARK Turn right at the ballfields parking lot and look for a sculpture of bunnies and a baseball mitt at the southwest corner of the ballfields, next to the parking lot entrance. Use the pedestrian signal here to cross 131st Ave. NE for a return to the park.

Exploration Ideas

- *What did you see in the red metal sculpture near the playground in Wilmot Gateway Park?*
- *What did you see growing in the farm fields?*
- *How many peace poles did you see? What are the different images on each one?*

Nearby Walks and Points of Interest

The Woodinville Heritage Museum has charming displays in an historic home, a short drive east at 14121 NE 171st St.

The 21 Acres Center at 13701 NE 171st St. offers walking paths (check for open hours), a farm market, tours, and programs related to local agriculture.

King County's Brightwater Center, a large wastewater treatment facility a few miles north, has a network of walking paths through forested and wetland areas that include a look at several pieces of public art.

Brightly painted, artistic peace poles are located around Woodinville. Look for them at Wilmot Gateway Park, at the 21 Acres Center, and at DeYoung Park, 13680 NE 175th St.

Check for Updated Information

. . . .

City of Woodinville: **https://www.ci.woodinville.wa.us/**

Woodinville Heritage Society: **https://www.woodinville-heritage.org/**

21 Acres Center: https://21**acres.org/**

Brightwater Center: **https://www.kingcounty.gov/services/environment/brightwater-center.aspx**

CENTRAL WALKS

→ BELLEVUE
→ ISSAQUAH
→ MEDINA
→ MERCER ISLAND
→ SAMMAMISH

In the midst of a rapidly growing urban core, it's possible to find oases of nature, pockets of history, and artworks that encourage new perceptions.

Bellevue's Downtown Park offers easy walking, with much nature and art to see.

BELLEVUE: DOWNTOWN

THE HEART OF A CITY

Walk through an art-filled park and the charm of Old Bellevue to a waterfront area that connects nature and history.

LENGTH: About 1.25 miles

DIFFICULTY RATING: Moderately Easy

SURFACES: Sidewalks downtown; gravel and paved pathways in Downtown Park. Gravel and paved pathways (some very steep), metal dock surface, and stairs at Meydenbauer Bay Park.

STARTING POINT: Downtown Park, 10201 NE 4th St., Bellevue, WA 98004

PARKING: Parking lot at Downtown Park; may be monitored on busy weekends to allow park users only. Street parking on Main St. and side streets. For Meydenbauer Bay Park, access the parking lot from 98th Ave. NE between NE 4th St. and NE 5th St.

PUBLIC TRANSIT: King County Metro

KIDS WILL ENJOY: Large Inspiration Playground designed for all abilities in Downtown Park; playground and beach at Meydenbauer Bay Park.

SERVICES ALONG ROUTE OR NEARBY: Restrooms located at Downtown and Meydenbauer Bay Parks. Restaurants, gas, and retail along Main St. and Bellevue Way.

Route Description

SOUTHWEST ENTRANCE TO BELLEVUE DOWNTOWN PARK, NE 1ST ST. AND 100TH AVE. NE Start at the entrance to the children's Inspiration Playground area; notice the leaf and insect design on the south arbor, and the colorful nature design used for donor recognition on the south fence. Inside the play area, look for very artistic play structures including a fanciful metal tree and a mosaic frog designed for exploration by the visually impaired. Restrooms located in this area.

Exit the play area to the north, walking under a metal arbor with a leaf design, noticing if it casts a shadow on the sidewalk. Just outside the north play area entrance, look for a large metal mobile sculpture.

Follow the paved pathway to the west of the sculpture or walk up the stairs to the east of the sculpture to reach the gravel circular path. Follow this path clockwise around the main park area, noticing the landscape architecture of the pond and waterfall, terraced lawn and seating area, and terraced stream.

In Bellevue's Downtown Park, many sculptures can be seen on the ground, but some can be seen only by looking up.

At the grand staircase at the north end of the park, go up the stairs for a high viewpoint of the park and a glimpse of Mt. Rainier when weather permits. Also notice the foundation remains and large trees at the center of the lawn that mark the site of Overlake Elementary School, which stood here from 1942 until 1986. A memorial to fallen soldiers from Bellevue is also located here.

Continue to follow the circular path clockwise, staying near the outer edge so you can spot the many pieces of public art that are tucked away among the side lawns and trees at the east side of the park. Take a detour from the main path to the formal rose and flower garden in the northeast corner of the park; look for a path leading east from the main trail. Restrooms located here.

Returning to the main circle path, continue clockwise and keep looking to your left for artworks on the east side of the park.

NE 1ST ST. AND 102ND AVE. NE When you reach the stairs at the south end of the park, cross NE 1st St. using the crosswalk on the east side of 102nd Ave. NE. Look for the utility box wrapped with historic photos of this area; another set of boxes is located at the southeast corner of Main St. and 100th Ave. NE.

Watch for informational signs about local history, such as this one on a building side in downtown Bellevue

102ND AVE. NE TO MAIN ST. Walk one block south to Main St. Turn left/east if you want to explore the full length of this historic commercial area (called Old Bellevue), or turn right/ west to continue this walk. Some historic and midcentury commercial and apartment buildings still remain; look for their interesting architecture as well as history signs tucked between the modern buildings.

MAIN ST. TO LAKE WASHINGTON BLVD. NE TO MEYDENBAUER BAY PARK At the west end of Main St., the street bears right and becomes Lake Washington Blvd. NE as you cross 100th Ave. NE. For the nature portion of this walk, continue west on Lake Washington Blvd. NE for one long block to the crosswalk at the east entrance to Meydenbauer Bay Park. Note: The walk into the park from this entrance involves a very steep sidewalk. For less steep access, drive to the Park's parking lot and walk into the west entrance.

Meydenbauer Bay Park in Bellevue offers a modern Lake Washington view in an historic setting.

MEYDENBAUER BAY PARK From the beach area, you have several options for exploration. Walk to the end of the dock to see the view of the lake and look for the metal sundial and sculptures of local birds.

Follow the sidewalk east of the beach area through a sculpture that reflects whale bones, a nod to the history of the whaling station building just east of the park. Read the history sign at the building's entry or visit the building if open; restrooms inside.

Returning to the main park area, look for metal oar sculptures on the upper sidewalk; an embedded fish design at the base has a riddle that will entertain older kids. Restrooms and picnic tables in this area.

Continue walking west past the playground to viewpoints with artistic designs in the metal fence panels. Look for additional sculptures scattered throughout the forested areas next to the sidewalk that leads to the parking lot.

To finish this walk, return to the main walkway and exit the park, turn right/east on Lake Washington Blvd. NE, then left/north on 100th Ave. NE to return to Downtown Park.

Exploration Ideas

- *In Downtown Park, did you see the artwork that looks like ordinary rocks?*
- *From the Meydenbauer Park dock, look around to see if you spot the birds in real life that you see in the artworks.*

- *How many utility boxes did you find in Old Bellevue that are wrapped with history photos and information?*
- *Can you imagine what activity happened at the whaling building in Meydenbauer Bay Park?*

Nearby Walks and Points of Interest

Bellevue Walk #2, in the Bellevue Botanical Garden, is approximately 2 miles east by car (see next walk)

Bellevue Arts Museum is located one block north of Downtown Park: **www.bellevuearts.org**

Many pieces of public art are located around downtown Bellevue; map available at: **http://www.visitbellevuewashington.com/includes/content/docs/media/Bellevue_Art_Map_Sections_Version.pdf**

Eastside Heritage Center publishes a brochure with a detailed history walking tour of downtown Bellevue: **https://www.eastsideheritagecenter.org/s/EH-WalkingTourBrochure-WEB.pdf**

Check for Updated Information

City of Bellevue Parks: **https://parks.bellevuewa.gov/parks-and-trails/parks/**

Artworks are often tucked into the trees at Bellevue Botanical Garden; keep your eyes open!

BELLEVUE #2: BELLEVUE BOTANICAL GARDEN

MORE THAN FLOWERS

Discover an extensive forest area, a suspension bridge, buildings of historical interest, and a growing collection of public art pieces.

LENGTH: About 1 mile

DIFFICULTY RATING: Moderate; some parts of the route involve noticeable uphill or downhill walking

SURFACES: Mostly gravel and dirt paths, some with exposed roots and optional stairs. Optional walk over suspension bridge with open slats on surface.

STARTING POINT: Bellevue Botanical Garden, 12001 Main St., Bellevue, WA 98005

PARKING: Parking lot at garden; follow signs to overflow parking on busy summer weekends.

PUBLIC TRANSIT: None nearby

KIDS WILL ENJOY: A large lawn area for play, the bounciness of a suspension bridge, and looking for tucked-away artworks, water features, and a "hobbit house."

SERVICES ALONG ROUTE OR NEARBY: Restrooms in Visitor Center and Shorts house. Coffee bar in Shorts house (seasonal/limited hours). Restaurants, gas, and retail along 120th Ave. NE and NE 8th St.

Route Description

MAIN GARDEN ENTRANCE As you walk from the parking lot to the visitor center, you're greeted by a colorful metal and glass sculpture next to the main entrance. On the west side of the entrance breezeway, turn right at the refreshing waterfall and follow the sidewalk past the gift shop and restrooms toward the Education Center.

EDUCATION CENTER TO SHARP CABIN Turn left and follow the gravel path west through the alpine and rock garden area. Continue west on the gravel path to see the small, historic Sharp cabin, which was moved to the site from its original farm location nearby and is now used as a meeting and work space. Learn more about the cabin and its family from the history sign located in the planting area on the north side of the building.

*The Sharp cabin is one sign of local farming
history at Bellevue Botanical Garden.*

PERENNIAL BEDS Follow the path to the west and south of
the cabin and enter the main lawn area. Look for one of the
small trails that lead to the perennial beds on the west side of
the lawn. Explore these plantings by looking for signs that you
can scan with your phone for more information.

MAIN LOOP TRAIL Follow the paths or use the stairs in the middle of the perennial beds to the main loop trail on the west boundary of the garden, then turn left/south. Notice the contrast of the planted areas to your left and the natural forest on your right. Take time to read the signs that showcase aspects of the garden then continue walking south. As you fully enter the forest, watch for a small opening to the left for an overlook of the pond with a carved stone bench for seating.

SOUTH LOOP TRAIL Return to the main loop trail and walk to the first junction, then turn right and follow the south trail as it wanders with slight uphill and downhill sections. At the clearings, imagine the farm that once was here and look for the concrete foundation remains for an old barn. Also look for the large beehive sculpture, made from reclaimed barn wood; be sure to go inside for an interesting light view if the sculpture's door is open.

RAVINE EXPERIENCE Continue on the south loop trail, following as it turns left/east and then left/north. At the sign for the Ravine Experience, turn right/east to reach the suspension bridge for a deep view into a forest ravine and creek below.

Important note: Bridge is very bouncy when people walk on it and the bridge surface has open slats that can make for difficult walking. The bridge leads to a circle of side paths in the forest that make an easy way to extend your walk. When ready, return to the south loop trail and turn right/north.

MAIN LOOP TRAIL At the junction with the main loop trail, turn right/east and take the first side path on the left to enter the pond view area. Continue left in this area to view a bronze sculpture of an owl in flight. Return to the main loop trail and turn left/north.

YAO JAPANESE GARDEN Turn right/east at the next side path and pass through the gate for the Yao Japanese Garden. Follow the circle path to see the full garden and carved stone lanterns.

MAIN LOOP TRAIL Exit the Yao garden and walk west on the main loop trail. Look for a boardwalk on the right for a viewing area of a small stream and waterfall. A history sign tells the story of how this private residential property became the Bellevue Botanical Garden. As you leave the stream area, look to the left for the metal leaf chair tucked into the trees, then look for a small trail to the right leading to a tiny "hobbit house" door that will delight children.

Continue on the main loop trail as it curves right/east until it crosses the waterfall and stream bridge and reaches the Tateuchi Pavilion, designed to represent a Japanese tea house. Look for more stone lanterns and a carved basalt stone bench in this area.

Follow the main loop trail to the east of the stream to reach the mid-century Shorts house and main lawn area. A coffee bar, restrooms, and atrium are located inside the house and tables on the patio make a nice spot for a break. On the east side of the house is a water feature and a bronze frog sculpture that will entertain children. From here, follow the path to the right to return to the garden entrance and parking lot.

Exploration Ideas

- Can you imagine what it would have been like to live as a family in the Sharp cabin?
- In the Japanese garden, look for stone lanterns: How many do you count?
- Did you find the hobbit house and the bronze frog sculpture?

Nearby Walks and Points of Interest

Bellevue #1: Downtown (see previous walk)

Check for Updated Information

Bellevue Botanical Garden: **www.bellevuebotanical.org**
City of Bellevue Parks: **https://parks.bellevuewa.gov/
parks-and-trails/parks/**
Eastside Heritage Center: **https://www.eastsideheri-
tagecenter.org/**

ELEVATION
109 Feet

ISSAQUAH

SEATTLE
42 Miles

The restored Issaquah train depot gives a sense of local logging, mining, and farming history.

ISSAQUAH

ART MEETS HISTORY MEETS SALMON

A loop route explores the art and history-filled downtown, a creekside park, and the popular salmon hatchery.

LENGTH: About 2.25 miles

DIFFICULTY RATING: Easy

SURFACES: Sidewalks, paved and gravel paths. Note: This walk has multiple trolley rail crossings that may be difficult for strollers and wheelchairs: look for alternate pathways nearby.

STARTING POINT: Issaquah Library, 10 W. Sunset Way, Issaquah, WA 98027

PARKING: Street parking along Front St., 1st Ave. S, and Rainier Ave. S. Public parking lot behind retail buildings on east side of Front St. and north of Sunset Way.

PUBLIC TRANSIT: King County Metro

KIDS WILL ENJOY: Viewing the train cars and taking the historic trolley ride (seasonal, weekends) at the train depot. Playground and large lawn areas at Confluence Park. Looking for salmon in Issaquah Creek from the bridge at Confluence Park and at the hatchery during the autumn spawning season.

SERVICES ALONG ROUTE OR NEARBY: Restrooms at library, Confluence Park, and hatchery. Restaurants, gas, and retail throughout downtown Issaquah.

Route Description

ISSAQUAH LIBRARY Begin the walk by looking around the library entrance; notice the animal and leaf prints in the concrete blocks and the metal bench at the southeast corner of the building with an artistic salmon design.

E SUNSET WAY AND FRONT ST. TO 1ST AVE. SE Walk east and cross Front St. At the northeast corner, notice the art image that wraps the traffic signal box.

Continue walking east on Sunset Way, passing by the historic Rollin' Log Tavern and Grand Central Hotel buildings. Just before the entrance road to the parking lot, stop and look south to find the painted mural that depicts Issaquah's logging history. (You'll see three more murals later in the walk.)

E SUNSET WAY AND 1ST AVE. SE Cross the parking lot entrance road, then use the crosswalk to cross Sunset Way going south and enter the grassy median between 1st Ave. S and Rainier Ave. S. Notice the sculpture of a long-time Issaquah city clerk who enjoyed this spot for reading.

1ST AVE. SE TO SE BUSH ST. Follow the sidewalk south, noticing more sculptures in the two blocks between Sunset Way and SE Bush St. Also on display are historic logging tools and equipment. The historic Gibson house is on the south side of 1st Ave. SE; the yellow house on the north side is a replica of another early home. Other vintage homes can be seen on neighboring streets.

SE BUSH ST. TO E SUNSET WAY/ ISSAQUAH CITY HALL Follow the sidewalk north to return to Sunset Way and cross to the plaza in front of Issaquah City Hall. A bronze eagle and salmon sculpture and a blue Moroccan door are located here.

PATH TO ISSAQUAH SENIOR CENTER AND ISSAQUAH TRAIN DEPOT Follow the sidewalk north until it becomes a paved pathway. At the first junction turn right and look at the multipart stone sculpture and the metal salmon ring sculpture near the entrance to the Issaquah Senior Center. Follow the sidewalk to the east side of the building and view another stone sculpture about salmon migration. Retrace your steps to the paved pathway, then cross the railroad tracks to visit the history displays at the train depot. Walk around the depot to view several information signs about area history.

Return to the paved pathway and walk north three blocks. Notice the painted sign on the back of the yellow building, a replica of historic advertising.

NE DOGWOOD ST. AND FRONT ST. N Just before the Dogwood St. intersection, take the small path to reach the sidewalk on the east side of Front St. and turn left; a multipart rock sculpture that represents Issaquah coal mining history is located at this corner; trolley tracks located here.

Walk south, looking at the horse sculpture made from repurposed tools and equipment parts. At the yellow building, visit the historic Hailstone Feed Store if open and look at the contemporary mural illustrating Issaquah life today.

FRONT ST. N TO NW GILMAN BLVD. Turn around and return to NE Dogwood St., then continue walking north on the east side of Front St. You'll see the historic Grange building your left and cross a bridge over the East Fork of Issaquah Creek.

After crossing Crescent Dr. NE, start looking for the multiple art pieces that honor the memory of McNugget, a popular rooster who lived for many years in the store parking lot. Then look west to view the murals on the east and north sides of the Darigold building, illustrating Issaquah agriculture history.

NW GILMAN BLVD. TO NW HOLLY ST. TO RAINIER BLVD. N. Walk north one block to NW Gilman Blvd. and look at the artwork on the traffic signal box located at the southeast corner.

Cross to the west side of Front St. and walk south for one-half block to NW Holly St. Turn right and walk three blocks to Rainier Blvd. N; trolley tracks located here.

Cross to the southeast corner, where you will have a partial view of Mt. Rainier if it's a sunny day. Cross west to the entrance of Confluence Park at the southwest corner of Rainier Blvd. N and NW Holly St. Notice the historic farmhouse on your left as you enter the park.

CONFLUENCE PARK Follow the gravel pathway on the north side of Confluence Park, then turn left at the junction to walk southwest toward the bridge. Notice the native plants along Issaquah Creek on your right.

Turn right at the access path and walk onto the bridge, noticing the artistic elements of crushed glass embedded in the walking surface and the metal elements at the bridge center. Stop and look at the views of Issaquah Creek, including migrating salmon in the autumn.

CONFLUENCE PARK TO RAINIER BLVD. N TO NW DOGWOOD ST. AND FRONT ST. N Return to the access path and walk east past the picnic shelter, then turn right at the sidewalk to walk south along Rainier Blvd. N, crossing another bridge over the East Fork of Issaquah Creek. At NW Dogwood St., cross to the west side of Front St. N and turn right. Look for the salmon carved in the stone bench just north of Village

Theatre. Continue to walk south for three blocks, noticing the many historic commercial buildings of old Issaquah.

FRONT ST. N AND W SUNSET WAY Continue south to the intersection of Front St. and Sunset Way. When you reach the library, notice the carved poetry stones and the second raven sculpture on the east side of the building. A third raven sculpture is located inside the library.

W SUNSET WAY TO ISSAQUAH SALMON HATCHERY Cross W Sunset Way to the south, then walk west two blocks to the entrance of the Issaquah Salmon Hatchery. Near the main building, look for an eagle and salmon sculpture carved from a tree trunk and the bronze sculptures of the hatchery mascots, Finley and Gilda. If the viewing room is open, watch the video presentation about the salmon migration and hatchery operations and history.

Follow the sound of water to walk on the bridge that crosses Issaquah Creek. This is a great spot to see salmon swimming upstream during the autumn spawning season; also notice the animal prints embedded in the concrete.

At the southwest end of the bridge, turn left to view the mural painted on the water tower about salmon migration. Be sure to view the mural from all sides. (You can avoid metal grates in this area by going south and east around the large holding pen.)

Walk to the south side of the holding pen for a close-up view of swimming salmon, then view the glass mosaic mural in this area that was created as a community art project.

Walk out of the viewing area at the west side, noticing the salmon design in the metal covers of the tree wells. Then look for the stone circle with a Native American story about the salmon journey. If the science center building is open, view the helpful exhibits; also look around the native plant gardens on the southeast side of the hatchery grounds.

Walk back across the bridge and exit the hatchery to return to the library starting point.

Exploration Ideas

- Did you find the three bronze ravens at the library? (Hint: Look above)

- Metal bicycle racks located throughout downtown have three different designs. Did you see all three?

- Some parts of the rock sculpture at Dogwood St. and Front St., N are located across the street and a bit south; can you spot them?

- What are all of the images you see in the painted murals around town?

Nearby Walks and Points of Interest

The Issaquah History Museums exhibits at the train depot and nearby Gilman Town Hall present details about the historic buildings along this walk.

Several walking trails connect downtown Issaquah with neighborhood and regional trails; look for trail signs while walking or download a map at: **https://www.issaquahwa.gov/trails**

Check for Updated Information

City of Issaquah: **https://www.issaquahwa.gov/**

City of Issaquah public art: **http://www.ci.issaquah.wa.us/index.aspx?NID=265**

Issaquah Library: **http://kcls.org/locations/1513/**

Issaquah History Museums: **https://www.issaquah-history.org/**

Issaquah Salmon Hatchery: **https://www.issaquahfish.org/**

Look for artistic designs in the structural elements and deck of the Confluence Park bridge in Issaquah.

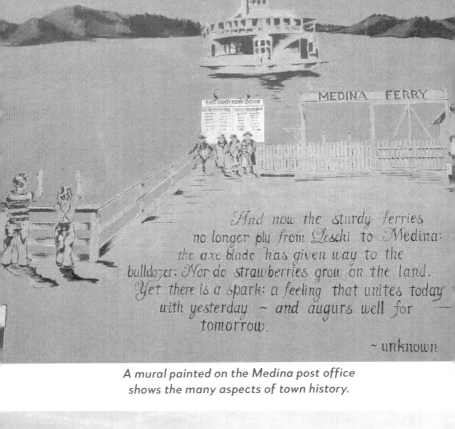

And now the sturdy ferries
no longer ply from Leschi to Medina:
the axe blade has given way to the
bulldozer; Nor do strawberries grow on the land.
Yet there is a spark: a feeling that unites today
with yesterday ~ and augurs well for
tomorrow.

~ unknown

*A mural painted on the Medina post office
shows the many aspects of town history.*

*Medina Beach Park is the place to imagine travelling to Seattle
by ferry before bridges were built over Lake Washington.*

MEDINA

See a hint of history while enjoying the same views as today's tech billionaires.

LENGTH: Less than .5 mile

DIFFICULTY RATING: Easy

SURFACES: Sidewalks (some steep), paved and gravel paths in the park; metal grated surface on the dock.

STARTING POINT: Medina Beach Park, 501 Evergreen Point Rd., Medina, WA 98039

PARKING: Designated street parking spots north of the park entrance; look for signs. Spots will fill quickly on nice days, especially in summer.

PUBLIC TRANSIT: None nearby

KIDS WILL ENJOY: Beach area with lake access

SERVICES ALONG ROUTE OR NEARBY: Restrooms in the City Hall building. Small store one block north of the park. Other retail, restaurants, and gas in downtown Bellevue.

Route Description

MEDINA BEACH PARK Use the sidewalk on the west side of Evergreen Point Rd. to reach the Medina Beach Park entrance. Walk south into the garden area at the southeast corner of the City Hall building, then to reach the pier that extends into Lake Washington, once the landing site of a ferry to Seattle.

Return to the gravel path in the garden area and follow it west and north to explore the park, including a small beach and swimming area with views of the Seattle skyline. Picnic tables, benches, and restrooms located here.

Follow the sidewalk uphill to return to Evergreen Point Rd. and turn left/north to the intersection with NE 8th St. Cross to the northeast corner and notice the historic Medina Grocery building. Continue walking to the north side of the post office to see an artistic mural that illustrates the history of the ferry landing as well as logging and farming in the area.

Exploration Ideas

- Can you imagine the ferry dock that once was here? What would it have been like to travel to Seattle by ferry instead of by car?

- What are all the different activities pictured in the town mural?

Nearby Walks and Points of Interest

Medina Park, located at 7789 NE 12th St., has a playground, ponds and lawn areas, and a picnic shelter with an interesting wood sculpture.

Check for Updated Info

City of Medina: **https://www.medina-wa.gov/index.asp**
Eastside Heritage Center; search for articles about historic ferry travel: **https://www.eastsideheritagecenter.org**

One of two beach areas that provide lake access at Luther Burbank Park on Mercer Island.

MERCER ISLAND

UNEXPECTED DISCOVERIES IN A LAKESIDE PARK

A large historic farm turned lakefront park offers a choice of scenic walks.

LENGTH: About 1.5 miles total; the north and south segments are approximately .75 miles each

DIFFICULTY RATING: Easy

SURFACES: Paved or gravel paths

STARTING POINT: North parking lot, Luther Bank Park, 2040 84th Ave. SE, Mercer Island, WA 98040

PARKING: Separate parking lots available for use while visiting Luther Burbank Park and Mercer Island Community & Event Center. The park has an additional parking lot at the south end; look for the entrance near the intersection of 84th Ave. SE and SE 26th St. Download and print a copy of the park trail map before your visit to help navigate the trails in case you must park in the south parking lot.

PUBLIC TRANSIT: No service directly to the park, although King County Metro serves the Mercer Island Transit Center about six blocks away. The walk between the park and the transit center involves significant uphill and downhill segments and extensive stairs.

KIDS WILL ENJOY: The park has a playground, two sandy beach areas with lake access, a large grassy playfield, and a grass-covered public artwork for exploration.

SERVICES ALONG ROUTE OR NEARBY: Restrooms located at Luther Burbank Park and Mercer Island Community & Event Center. Restaurants, gas, and retail throughout the downtown area.

Route Description

LUTHER BURBANK PARK From the north parking lot, look for the main entry path under the covered walkway. Walk east toward the historic brick building, noticing the mural of local birds on the west wall of the tennis courts as you pass by. Restrooms located between the playground and the tennis courts.

NORTH SEGMENT The large brick building was once the dormitory when the park was a working farm and residential school for children considered delinquent and placed in state care. Look for the bronze rooster sculpture at the southwest corner and the history sign at the northwest corner; also notice the building's many architectural details. Picnic tables and benches in the grassy area to the north provide views of Lake Washington.

The historic dormitory building dates from when Luther Burbank Park on Mercer Island was a residential school and farm for children in state care.

Continue the walk northward by following the paved pathway as it curves left/west, then turn right/north at the junction. When you reach the off-leash dog area, pet the bronze dog sculpture outside the fence. Notice the extensive growth of wild roses, either in bloom or as rose hips. When you reach the concrete foundations, imagine the barns that once stood here.

Continue on the paved path to the open grassy area and a small sandy beach with lake access and views of Seattle and Bellevue. Picnic tables here.

Walk back to the parking lot along the paved path or on the gravel path on the west side of the barn foundations. Notice the wetland area on the west side of this path.

To extend your walk, return to the brick building and follow the route description below for the south segment.

SOUTH SEGMENT Walk south through the playground and continue on the dirt path. Look for a side path to the left that goes downhill to the historic boiler plant building and to walk on the dock that extends into the lake.

Return uphill to the main path by turning left/south as you face the boiler plant building. Continue south on the main trail past a large grassy area to your right/west. At the junction, veer left to stay on the main trail.

After a short distance, turn left/east and walk slightly downhill to a small swimming beach. Restrooms, picnic tables, and a play structure are in this area.

To the west of the beach area, notice the grassy hills of the landscape art installation, which kids will enjoy exploring.

Facing the lake from here, return to the main path and turn left/ north to walk back through the playground, noticing the mosaic mural near the restrooms. Turn left at the covered walkway to reach the north parking lot.

This landscape feature at Mercer Island's Luther Burbank Park provides a new perspective on public art and a fun area for kids to explore.

Exploration Ideas

- *Can you imagine this area when it was a working farm? What do you think the barns looked like and what did they hold?*

- *What do you think the artist was trying to express with the large grass landscape artwork? What would you use this area for?*

- *What are the different birds and designs that you see in the painted and mosaic murals?*

Nearby Walks and Points of Interest

Mercer Island Community & Event Center hosts rotating art exhibits in the main level lobby area. The lobby staircase has carved metal panels with unique designs of fruit, flowers, greenery, and animals.

Several sculptures are installed as an outdoor exhibit in the park area on top of the I-90 freeway, along Sunset Highway between 77th Ave. SE and 80th Ave. SE.

Check for Updated Info

Luther Burbank Park trail map: **https://www.mercergov.org/ Page.asp?NavID=1138**

Mercer Island Community & Event Center: **https://www. mercergov.org/Page.asp?NavID=1951**

City of Mercer Island outdoor sculpture exhibit: **http://www. mercergov.org/Page.asp?NavID=3179**

Mercer Island Historical Society: **http://www.mercerisland-history.org/**

Detailed view of a totem pole at
Beaver Lake Park in Sammamish.

SAMMAMISH

AN ESCAPE FROM THE CITY

Enjoy lake access, forest trails, hints of history, and art that reflects native heritage.

LENGTH: About 1 mile

DIFFICULTY RATING: Easy

SURFACES: Paved, bark, or gravel paths

STARTING POINT: Lodge at Beaver Lake Park, 25201 SE 24th St., Sammamish, WA 98074

PARKING: Park parking lot; often fills to capacity on warm days

PUBLIC TRANSIT: None nearby

KIDS WILL ENJOY: Lawn and beach areas for play

SERVICES ALONG ROUTE OR NEARBY: Restrooms located at the rear of Beaver Lake Lodge. Restaurants, gas, and retail along 228th Ave. SE.

Route Description

BEAVER LAKE LODGE TO PICNIC PAVILION From the parking lot, walk to Beaver Lake Lodge, the large log cabin style building near the park entrance. If the Lodge is open, notice the log walls and stone fireplace for a feeling of the building's history. This is the only structure that remains from the park's early days as a summer vacation resort, although it has been remodeled and expanded.

From the Lodge's front porch, follow the path to the right/ southeast, toward the lake and picnic pavilion. At the junction, continue right on the paved path to the large totem pole in the grassy area; the metal sign behind the pole tells the story of its figures.

PICNIC PAVILION TO LAKE Continue on the path to the picnic pavilion. Inside are three carved panels in a native design. (During the summer weekends, the pavilion is typically reserved for groups. Please don't enter if a group is using it without asking permission.)

Walk through the pavilion to the lakeshore. When the leaves are off the trees, you can see some of the older cabins mixed in with modern homes on the opposite shore. Enjoy the view of water, trees and lily pads.

Beaver Lake offers peaceful views in Sammamish to summer resort visitors of the past and park visitors of today.

LAWN AREA TO FOREST PATH To resume the walk, take the gravel path to the left when you're facing the picnic pavilion with your back to the lake. After a short walk, you can enjoy another totem pole.

Follow the gravel path as it curves to the right. You'll see more areas with picnic tables and lake access to stop for a rest or lunch.

Cross the bridge and follow the very narrow path to the left if you want a small view of Long Lake. Return back over the bridge, then take an immediate left onto a dirt path to continue walking in the forest.

Just past the second bridge, turn right at the T junction to a straight, open stretch of trail. If you're ready for a break, a bench provides a nice resting stop.

FOREST PATH TO PARKING LOT Follow the trail as it continues past the park maintenance facility then to the parking lot.

Exploration Ideas

- *In the first totem pole, do you recognize the salmon, bear, and eagle figures? What other creatures do you see? In the second totem pole, how many beavers do you see?*

- *On the forest trail, notice the different trees, shrubs, native wildflowers, and ferns. Listen to the birds, look for mushrooms and moss, smell the cedar and pine and moisture. As you cross the two wood puncheon bridges, look for animal tracks in the mud around you. Look at the height of the trees, then look at the forest floor. Can you see the stumps of bigger trees that were once logged here?*

Nearby Walks and Points of Interest

Beaver Lake Park has a several other trails that can extend this walk. Nearby Beaver Lake Preserve offers an easy trail walk through the forest and a small viewing area of Beaver Lake.

The traffic signal box at the northeast corner of 228th Ave. SE and SE 24th St. has a wrap with historic photos and information about Sammamish schools in the early 20th century. Find background information and locations at: **http://www.hshedd.com/claradellshedd/pages/projectbox.html**

Check for Updated Information

Beaver Lake Park: **https://www.sammamish.us/parks-recreation/parks-trails/beaver-lake-park/**
Beaver Lake Preserve: **https://www.sammamish.us/parks-recreation/parks-trails/beaver-lake-preserve/**
City of Sammamish: **https://www.sammamish.us/**
Sammamish Heritage Society: **www.sammamishheritage.org** and History Link article about Beaver Lake Resort history: **https://www.historylink.org/File/8183**

SOUTHERN WALKS

→ MAPLE VALLEY
→ NEWCASTLE
→ RENTON

Rich history combines with abundant nature and distinctive art for unexpected learning and discovery.

Lake Wilderness Park in Maple Valley offers many interesting natural, artistic, and historic features to explore.

MAPLE VALLEY

A LAKE, A GARDEN, & A STEP BACK IN TIME

This two-part route explores a lakeside park and garden area, then follows a railway path to the local history museum.

LENGTH: Arboretum & Lake Wilderness Park loop: About 1.25 miles. Arboretum to Maple Valley History Museum: About 1 mile round-trip

DIFFICULTY RATING: Easy

SURFACES: Gravel and dirt paths

STARTING POINT: Lake Wilderness Park, 22500 SE 248th St., Maple Valley, WA 98038

PARKING: *Lake Wilderness Park:* Use the Arboretum lot; enter from SE 248th St. Additional parking lots near the Lodge and at the main park entrance, located to the south on 224th Ave. SE

Maple Valley History Museum: Use the parking lot at the Maple Valley Community Center, 22010 SE 248th St., Maple Valley, WA 98038

PUBLIC TRANSIT: None nearby

KIDS WILL ENJOY: In the Arboretum, look for the Children's Discovery Forest on the west side of the nursery. The park offers a swimming beach and large lawn areas. At the Museum, kids can explore the re-created general store and an historic fire engine.

SERVICES ALONG ROUTE OR NEARBY: Restrooms located throughout the park and at the history museum. Restaurants, gas, and retail approximately one mile north on Witte Rd. and Highway 169.

Route Description

LAKE WILDERNESS PARK ARBORETUM Begin at the southwest corner of the Lake Wilderness Arboretum, where you'll find numerous gravel and dirt trails and information signs to guide you through the planted areas. Of particular interest is the Tribal Life Trail, which presents extensive information about the use of local plants by native peoples. When you emerge from the east end of this trail, look for two totem poles and a gazebo in the lawn area.

Continue following the trails east past the nursery, taking time to enjoy the flower garden area. Look for a small pond with a sculptural stone bridge.

LAKE WILDERNESS PARK When you reach the lodge with its midcentury modern architecture, look for the information sign at the west entrance about this area's former use as a vacation resort.

At the south side of the lodge, look for the trellis entrance to the large lawn area with an untitled bronze sculpture. A small swimming beach, picnic tables, restrooms, and fishing pier are located here. Walk along the lake shore, reading information signs about the area's history involving railroads, homesteading, logging, and coal mining.

MAPLE VALLEY HISTORY MUSEUM If you're a history buff, plan to visit on an open day at the Maple Valley History Museum, a collection of buildings a few blocks west of the park. Even if the museum isn't open, you can get a sense of local history by walking around the exterior of the General Store building and looking at the outdoor exhibits and history signs. The museum is adjacent to the Maple Valley Community Center; look for an artistic seating bench at this building's south entrance.

To reach the museum, follow the park trails to return to your car and drive west on SE 248th St. to the Maple Valley Community Center entrance at the northeast corner of the traffic circle at Witte Rd. As an alternative, reach the museum by walking west on the Green to Cedar Rivers Trail, which you can access by one of several paths on the north side of the Arboretum. This former railroad route is wide and flat, with a gravel surface; watch and listen for bicyclists. Return to your car on this trail when you have finished visiting the History Museum.

Exploration Ideas

- *In the Children's Discovery Forest, did you find the whimsically painted mailbox, kid-size seating areas, and multiple birdhouses?*

- *What did you learn about daily living from the signs along the Tribal Life Trail? About historic living and work activity from the signs along the lake?*

- *Can you imagine shopping in the General Store at the History Museum?*

Nearby Walks and Points Of Interest

Several pieces of public art are installed at the Maple Valley Library, located on the northwest corner of the traffic circle at Witte Rd. and SE 248th St.

The Green to Cedar Rivers Trail is a regional path that continues east and west from Lake Wilderness Park. You can extend your walk along this trail, or by following the neighborhood trails that extend up the hill north of the park.

Check for Updated Info

Lake Wilderness Park: **https://www.maplevalleywa.gov/ departments-services/parks-recreation/parks-and-trails/ lake-wilderness-park**
Maple Valley History Museum: **http://www.maplevalleyhis- torical.com/**
Maple Valley Library: **https://kcls.org/locations/1527/**
Green to Cedar Rivers Trail: **https://www.kingcounty.gov/ services/parks-recreation/parks/trails/regional-trails/ popular-trails/green-to-cedar.aspx**

The pioneer cemetery in Newcastle is rarely open, but the history sign outside presents a view into the town's early years.

NEWCASTLE

NATURE & REMEMBRANCE

*A pleasant park leads to lake access and
an historic pioneer cemetery.*

LENGTH: About 1 mile

DIFFICULTY RATING: Easy

SURFACES: Paved or gravel paths, paved street

STARTING POINT: Lake Boren Park, 13058 SE 84th Way,
Newcastle, WA 98056

PARKING: Parking lot at south end of Lake Boren Park;
enter from SE 84th Way

PUBLIC TRANSIT: King County Metro

KIDS WILL ENJOY: A grassy area, lake access, and a playground

SERVICES ALONG ROUTE OR NEARBY: Restrooms located
at Lake Boren Park. Restaurants, gas, and retail located in a
commercial area about 1 mile north of the park.

Route Description

LAKE BOREN PARK Start at the park entrance pathway from the south parking lot, near the restrooms and tennis courts. A map display next to the tennis courts shows other walking trails in the area; you can also download this map from the Newcastle trails website: **http://newcastletrails.org/**.

Follow the path as it proceeds north along the eastern edge of the park, enjoying the views of the open lawn areas and a mix of mature trees. As you approach the lake, look for an area of boulders on your right.

Follow the path as it continues left/northwest, getting your first access to Lake Boren. Enjoy the shoreline, then return to the path and turn right/west to continue.

At the junction, turn right/north and walk onto the pier for a full view of the lake. When you're ready, return to the main path and turn right/southwest.

LAKE BOREN PARK TO NEWCASTLE CEMETERY At the next junction, follow a small trail uphill, then veer right/northwest and follow the signs to enter the street (no sign) and walk north to the entrance of the historic Newcastle Cemetery entrance. Look for the fenced area on the hillside to your left, walking past the entrance to the sign that explains the cemetery's history. The cemetery is closed to the public except for the annual Newcastle Days festival in early September. If the cemetery isn't open, look up at the mature trees and imagine the peace of being buried there as a town pioneer.

NEWCASTLE CEMETERY TO LAKE BOREN PARK Go back on the street to return to Lake Boren Park and the main path on the side of the maintenance building. Follow this path south as it goes on a slight uphill along the west side of the park. Benches and picnic tables along this path offer a good rest stop.

Continue south past the playground to the parking lot. Take a moment to walk through the fuchsia garden near the park entrance and notice which plants are in bloom.

A note about public art: As of mid-2019, there were no public art installations in Lake Boren Park. The Newcastle Library has several artworks, and an artistic monument that commemorates coal mining in the area is located at the corner of 132nd Pl. SE and Newcastle Commons Dr. in the Newcastle Commons development, about one mile north of the park.

A brick monument commemorates the coal
mining history of Newcastle.

Exploration Ideas

- Could the large boulders be remnants of retreating
  glaciers in the Ice Age?
- When walking on the west side of the park, notice
  the new view of the areas you saw on the first part
  of the walk.

Nearby Walks and Points of Interest

For walks that present a deeper view into the area's coal mining past, explore the trails of nearby Cougar Mountain Regional Park: **https://www.kingcounty.gov/services/parks-rec-reation/parks/parks-and-natural-lands/popular-parks/cougar.aspx**

Check for Updated Info

Newcastle trail map and guides: **http://newcastletrails.org/**
City of Newcastle: **http://www.newcastlewa.gov**
Newcastle Historical Society: **https://www.newcastlewa-history.org/**
Newcastle Library: **http://kcls.org/locations/1564**

The art deco design of the Renton History Museum gives a view of historic architecture to complement the informative exhibits inside

RENTON

A short walk guides you to the unique architecture of a library built over a river and an art deco fire station.

LENGTH: About .25 mile

DIFFICULTY RATING: Easy

SURFACES: Sidewalks

STARTING POINT: Renton Library, 100 Mill Ave. S, Renton, WA 98057

PARKING: Public parking lot on south side of building at 200 Mill Ave. S

PUBLIC TRANSIT: King County Metro

KIDS WILL ENJOY: Looking into the river at the library and the museum exhibits of early community life.

SERVICES ALONG ROUTE OR NEARBY: Restrooms at library and history museum. Restaurants, gas, and retail throughout downtown area.

Route Description

RENTON LIBRARY Starting on the south side of the library, notice the small bronze sculpture of a reading boy. Follow the sidewalk on the east side of the building and look over the railing for a view of the Cedar River. During the fall months, you may see migrating salmon swimming upstream. Go inside the library for more art installations and another view of the river from the reading area on the west side of the building.

The Renton Library offers the unique and exciting view of an over-the-river building.

RENTON LIBRARY TO MILL AVE. AND BRONSON WAY TO RENTON HISTORY MUSEUM Exit the library and walk to the intersection of Mill Ave. and Bronson Way, using the stoplight to cross to the west side. Turn left to walk south on Mill Ave. two blocks to the small park area on the north side of the Renton History Museum. Look at the history display about logging operations and the 1910 Chief Sealth water fountain.

Located at 235 Mill Ave. S., the museum is housed in the city's first fire station, built in 1942 and one of the last remaining art deco stations in the Seattle area. Displays illustrate local history from native settlement to development of Renton as a farming, logging, and coal mining town and eventually major facilities for Boeing.

On the south side of the museum is a small park and plaza that honors local veterans.

RENTON HISTORY MUSEUM TO MILL AVE. AND BRONSON WAY As you walk back to the Bronson Way intersection, notice the enameled metal mural on the southeast side of the modern fire station. At the traffic light, cross Mill Ave. to return to the library and parking lot.

Exploration Ideas

- *Which artworks did you find inside the library?*
- *Which aspects of early Renton history did you find most interesting? How was life in times past different from and the same as today?*

Nearby Walks and Points of Interest

Several pieces of public art are installed throughout the downtown area; more information on the works and their locations is available at: **https://rentonwa.gov/city_hall/ community_services/recreation_and_neighborhoods/ recreation/arts_and_entertainment/renton_s_public_art**

A walk along the Lake Washington shoreline with a public art installation and botanical information signs is available at Gene Coulon Park, a short drive north of the downtown area: **https://rentonwa.gov/city_hall/commu- nity_services/parks_and_trails/find_a_park_or_trail/ gene_coulon_memorial_beach_park**

Check for Updated Information

City of Renton: **https://www.rentonwa.gov/**
Renton Library: **https://kcls.org/locations/1556/**
Renton History Museum: **www.rentonhistory.org**

Watch for artistic designs embedded in sidewalks and crosswalks

SNOQUALMIE VALLEY WALKS

→ CARNATION
→ DUVALL
→ FALL CITY
→ NORTH BEND
→ SNOQUALMIE

From farmland to riversides, historic train depots to mountain views, the Snoqualmie Valley offers a varied mix of interesting walks.

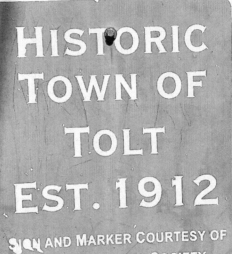

TOLT

HISTORIC TOWN OF TOLT EST. 1912

SIGN AND MARKER COURTESY OF
TOLT HISTORICAL SOCIETY
AND CITY OF CARNATION

The "Welcome to Tolt" monument reflects
the historic name of Carnation

CARNATION

A TOWN & COUNTRY WALK

*A quiet country town offers many discoveries
and varied scenery for a pleasant walk.*

LENGTH: About 1.25 miles

DIFFICULTY RATING: Easy

SURFACES: Sidewalks and gravel paths; slatted wood surface on the park bridge

STARTING POINT: Carnation Library, 4804 Tolt Ave., Carnation, WA 98014

PARKING: On-street parking on Tolt Ave.

PUBLIC TRANSIT: Snoqualmie Valley Transit

KIDS WILL ENJOY: Tolt McDonald Park, which has a suspension bridge, large grassy areas, and a playground.

SERVICES ALONG ROUTE OR NEARBY: Restrooms at library and Tolt McDonald Park. Restaurants, gas, and retail along Tolt Ave.

Route Description

CARNATION LIBRARY At the library entrance, notice the large table and lamp artwork, then view the painted wood panel with a Northwest native design on the west side of the building. You can see more public art inside the library during open hours.

This restored barn in Tolt McDonald Park provides a vivid reminder of Carnation's farming history

TOLT AVE. TO BIRD ST. From the library, walk south on the east side of Tolt Ave., noticing the historic commercial buildings on the main street and vintage homes on the side streets. Just before Bird St. is a small garden area with benches, called Tolt Town Commons. The bus shelter next to this area has interesting artwork.

TOLT AVE. TO ENTWISTLE ST. Continue south on Tolt Ave. to the stoplight at Entwistle St. Cross to the west side of Tolt Ave. Walk west on Entwistle approximately three blocks.

ENTWISTLE ST. TO LARSON AVE. Where the street turns left to become Larson Ave., look for a sign marking the trail to Tolt McDonald Park. It's a gravel trail on the north side of the public works building. As you enter the trail, enjoy the farmland views.

Enjoy a peaceful riverside resting spot at Tolt McDonald Park in Carnation.

TOLT MCDONALD PARK Stay on the trail as it turns left/south towards Tolt McDonald Park. Walk past the playground area and softball field. Turn right at the map kiosk just before the park entrance road and walk across the parking lot. At the park ranger's house, take a slight left and walk along the roadside to the grassy area on the right, with an old red barn converted to a covered picnic space. Portable toilets are located next to the barn.

Return to the roadway, turn right and walk across another parking lot and past the flagpole to the path for the suspension bridge. Note: The bridge has open wooden slats and can be very bouncy. At the bridge midpoint, turn north for a nice view of the Snoqualmie River. At the west end of the bridge, turn right for trails that pass along the river or turn left for a bench with a good river view.

Return to the library by retracing your route, but this time notice the distant Cascade views to the east at various points along the way.

TOLT AVE. TO ENTWISTLE ST. Walk along the west side of Tolt Ave. to explore the local businesses as you return to your car or starting point.

Exploration Ideas

- *Can you imagine this area when it had more farms? When it was covered with trees?*

- *Look at the art in the bus shelter on the west side of Tolt Town Commons; what themes do you see?*

- *On the suspension bridge, look for a sign and viewer to learn more about the history of the Tolt Bridge to the south.*

- *On the return route, look for logging history photos painted as murals on the side of buildings along Tolt Ave.*

Nearby Walks and Points of Interest

Tolt McDonald Park has an extensive trail system in the woods and along the river; check the website below for a map. The Snoqualmie Valley Trail passes through Carnation a few blocks east of Tolt Ave.

Carnation history walking tour itinerary: **https://savorsno-qualmievalley.org/itinerary/carnation-historic-walking-tour/**

The Tolt Historical Society Museum is located at Carnation Tree Farm, 31523 NE 40th St., Carnation; check website for open hours. The museum is a short walk from Tolt McDonald Park, but the road has limited sidewalks so you may find it easier to move your car and park at the museum.

Carnation Farms is an historic dairy farm that now operates as a nonprofit organic agriculture center. Offers periodic walking tours of the farm's history and nature.

Check For Updated Info

City of Carnation: **https://www.carnationwa.gov/**
Carnation Library: **http://kcls.org/locations/1496/**
Carnation Farms: **www.carnationfarms.org**
King County Parks: **https://www.kingcounty.gov/services/parks-recreation/parks/parks-and-natural-lands/popu-lar-parks/toltmacdonald.aspx**
Tolt Historical Society: **http://tolthistoricalsociety.org/**

HISTORIC RAILROAD

BUILT IN

1911

DEPOT

CITY OF DUVALL LANDMARK

FORMERLY CHICAGO MILWAUKEE ST. PAUL & PACIFIC RAILROAD
DONATED BY RAY & TOVE BURHEN 2001

*The historic Duvall depot is a great place to imagine
train travel through the Snoqualmie Valley.*

DUVALL

A RIVER TOWN OF HISTORY & ART

A small, art-filled community maintains its history alongside the Snoqualmie River.

LENGTH: About 1.25 miles

DIFFICULTY RATING: Moderately Easy; steep hill between Main St. and McCormick Park

SURFACES: Sidewalks downtown and in depot area; gravel and dirt paths in McCormick Park

STARTING POINT: Duvall Library, 15508 Main St. NE, Duvall, WA 98019

PARKING: Parking lot at entrance to McCormick Park; street parking on Main St. and side streets

PUBLIC TRANSIT: Snoqualmie Valley Transit

KIDS WILL ENJOY: Imagining train travel at the depot; a small sandy beach and large lawn areas along the river at McCormick Park

SERVICES ALONG ROUTE OR NEARBY: Restrooms located at the entrance to McCormick Park and at library. Restaurants, gas, and retail along Main St.

Route Description

. . . .

DUVALL LIBRARY/MAIN ST. Start at the entrance to the Duvall Library. Notice several art pieces here: A stylish bike rack, an artistic wrap around the utility box, and a metal sculpture in the planting area. If the library is open, go inside to look at the wood sculpture in the center of the reading area and other indoor artworks.

From the library, walk north on the east side of Main St., noticing the historic buildings on both sides of the street. Detailed information about these buildings is available in this history walking tour itinerary: **https://savorsnoqualmievalley.org/ itinerary/duvall-historic-walking-tour/**

Also start looking for two types of artwork along Main St. that illustrate local history and nature. First are 12 metal benches.

Second are the 10 sets of carved cedar wood panels hanging on streetlight posts. For details about the panel artists and images, download: **http://savorsnoqualmievalley.org/ itinerary/self-guided-art-tour-historic-duvall/**

*Duvall is full of public art, including carved
panels on Main Street lamp posts.*

MAIN ST. TO VIRGINIA ST./WOODINVILLE-DUVALL RD.
When you reach the stoplight at the intersection of Main St. and Virginia St./Woodinville-Duvall Rd., continue north of the crosswalk and go one block to see the pair of wood panels at the north entrance to town.

Return to the Woodinville-Duvall Rd. intersection and cross to the west side of Main St. Walk south along the west side of Main St. noticing more historic buildings, metal benches, and wood panels with different designs. Also notice the carved stone benches outside the red shingle building, which previously housed the town's library. Check for an art gallery inside Duvall City Hall, at the corner of Main St. and NE Stella St.

MAIN ST. AND BUHREN WAY When you reach the stoplight at the intersection of Main St. and Buhren Way continue south through the crosswalk and go one block to see the wood panels at the south entrance to town.

BUHREN WAY TO MCCORMICK PARK Return to Buhren Way, cross to the north side of the street and turn left (downhill). Pass under the gateway arch that notes Duvall's centennial (1913-2013).

Walk down the hill noting the three sculptures that present elements of the local community, then walk under the arbor to enter McCormick Park.

A walk through Duvall's McCormick Park brings views of the Snoqualmie River and open meadows.

MCCORMICK PARK You'll see the train depot immediately on your left. Although it is the historic depot for Duvall, this is not its original location. When the railroad was active, the depot was located near the tracks, which ran on what is now the Snoqualmie Valley Trail, the flat walking and biking path to the west of this site.

For the nature experience of this walk, follow the sidewalk on the north side of the depot, then take a slight right when you reach the gravel path. Look for the sign pointing left/downhill to the continuation of McCormick Park, and walk through the grassy area until you reach a small sandy beach with access to the Snoqualmie River.

Follow the path south along the river until you reach a large grassy area. The picnic tables and benches here and in the beach area make a good spot for lunch or a break, and provide a view of farm buildings on the other side of the river.

To finish the walk, follow the trail on the north side of the grassy area, heading east away from the river. Turn left/north when you reach the Snoqualmie Valley Trail, then right/east on the small sidewalk next to the depot, which you can follow uphill on Buhren Way to return to the library.

Exploration Ideas

- *Play "I Spy" to find the many artistic benches and carved wood panels along Main St. How many can you count?*

- *Look up at the McCormick Park entrance arbor: Can you see how it is made from old railroad ties and timbers?*

- *If the depot isn't being used for an event, stand on the porch and imagine what your travels might have been like in the town's early days.*

Nearby Walks and Points of Interest

The Snoqualmie Valley Trail runs through McCormick Park. This trail follows the former railroad line along the Snoqualmie River and through the countryside for miles in either direction.

The historic Dougherty farmstead is located approximately one-half mile north of downtown (best accessed by car). Check the Duvall Historical Society website for open hours.

Check for Updated Info

City of Duvall: **https://www.duvallwa.gov/186/Experience-Duvall**
Duvall Historical Society: **https://www.duvallhistorical-society.org/**
Duvall Library: **http://kcls.org/locations/1503/**

Fall City ... history lives here

Centennial Plate, 1985

Fall City Methodist Church, built 189

The church was established in 1885 by "Brother Mac," a traveling Methodist Episcopal minister. The original part of the present church building (above, right) was built in 1899 by the Fall City Baptists and sat across the street (Main Street, now 337th SE) to the west. The Baptists intended for the church to be used by other groups, and the Methodists gladly shared the building, having lost their earlier church. (See link bel for more early history.) By 1919, Baptist membership had declined, and the building was sold to the local Methodists for $250.

About 1927, the Methodists bought the property across the street t the east, and in 1929, the church was moved to its current location and turned to keep the entrance on Main Street. In the late 1950s and 196 additions and remodeling brought the building to its present configura

FALL CITY
HISTORICAL SOCIETY

4 CULTURE

FALL CITY

THE CHARM OF A VILLAGE

A small-town loop route offers a sense of discovering hidden historic and artistic treasures.

LENGTH: About 1 mile

DIFFICULTY RATING: Moderately Easy

SURFACES: Some sidewalks, but most of the walk is on gravel road shoulders and along paved streets

STARTING POINT: Southeast corner of Redmond-Fall City Rd. and 337th Pl. SE.

PARKING: Street parking on Redmond-Fall City Rd. and side streets

PUBLIC TRANSIT: King County Metro

KIDS WILL ENJOY: Identifying the symbols on the historic totem pole, lawn areas in the riverside park

SERVICES ALONG ROUTE OR NEARBY: Restrooms located at the library. Restaurants, gas, and retail along Redmond-Fall City Rd. SE and Preston-Fall City Rd. SE.

Route Description

REDMOND-FALL CITY RD. SE AND 337TH PL. SE This walk starts with a piece of public art: The river stone sculpture at the southeast corner of Redmond-Fall City Rd. SE and 337th Pl. SE Walk one block south on 337th Pl. SE, noticing the historic street names on the signs.

337TH PL. SE TO SE 43RD ST. Three historic buildings are in the next block: The Masonic Lodge at the corner of SE 43rd St., the Neighbor-Bennett House, and the United Methodist Church. Take time to read the history signs at each location.

337TH PL. SE TO SE 43RD PL. Continue south one block and turn left at SE 43rd Pl. for a walk through an older residential neighborhood with many vintage cottages and farmhouse-style homes. Keep your eye out for signs that present the history of this neighborhood.

SE 43RD PL. TO 338TH PL. SE TO 44TH PL. SE Walk one block east and turn right/south on 338th Pl. SE Walk one block south, then right/west on 44th Pl. SE. Note the old trees, rose bushes, and other plantings in the gardens as well as old garages and side buildings.

44TH PL. SE TO 336TH PL. SE Continue west on 44th Pl. SE for two blocks, then turn right on 336th Pl. SE. Look for the history sign about school buildings and locations in the community's early days.

336TH PL. SE TO SE 43RD PL. TO 335TH PL. SE Continue north for two blocks, then turn left/west on SE 43rd Pl. At the southwest corner of 335th Pl. SE, look for the eagles and nest carved into a tree stump, located in a private yard.

335TH PL. SE TO REDMOND-FALL CITY RD. Turn right/north on 335th Pl. SE and walk one block to see the historic home with a sign at the corner of Redmond-Fall City Rd.

Turn left/west on Redmond-Fall City Rd. and stay on the sidewalk for the Fall City Library. Look for the wire globe sculpture at the northwest corner of the library lawn, as well as the lighted message display visible through the windows. Other artworks are located inside the library, as well as restrooms.

REDMOND-FALL CITY RD. TO SE 42ND ST. From the library, use the crosswalk to cross Fir St. and head west on SE 42nd St. Cross to the north at the next crosswalk for a close look at the old brick gymnasium, the historic part of Fall City Elementary School; history sign located here.

TOTEM GARDEN Return to the walking path on the south side of the street. At Fir St., cross to the library, then cross SE 42nd Pl. (no crosswalk) to the small Totem Garden. Enjoy the garden area and read the history sign near the bench to learn about this historic artwork. Sit here for a good look upward at the totem pole.

REDMOND-FALL CITY RD. TO 335TH PL. SE Exit the garden area east of the bench and cross SE 42nd Pl. to the library (no crosswalk). Go one block east to cross Redmond-Fall City Rd. at the crosswalk on the northeast corner of 335th Pl. SE.

QUIGLEY PARK Enter the park picnic area next to the Snoqualmie River. This area makes a nice spot for enjoying the river views and to look for the nature and history signs next to the river bank. Also look at the three-column rock sculpture of migrating salmon in this area. Continue walking east along the river and notice the valley heritage sign near the corner of 336th Pl. SE.

*Quigley Park in Fall City offers a scenic
view of the Snoqualmie River.*

Exploration Ideas

- *How many symbols can you see on the totem pole? Compare your answers to the interpretive sign.*
- *Learn more about Snoqualmie Valley history on the two heritage signs in Quigley Park.*

Nearby Walks and Points of Interest

For an optional extension to this walk, at the east end of Quigley Park a narrow paved pathway on the west side of the bridge and roundabout leads to the gravel parking lot for Hop Kiln Park, corner of Carnation-Fall City Rd. SE and Neale Rd. Look for the gravel trails that lead to an historic storage building for the hops previously grown in this area.

The Snoqualmie Valley Trail passes on the east side of Highway 203; check for the nearest parking and access point: **http:// savorsnoqualmievalley.org/wp-content/uploads/2018/04/ Snoqualmie-Valley-Trail-Map-web..pdf**

Check for Updated Info

Fall City Arts: **https://www.fallcityarts.com/**
Fall City Library: **http://kcls.org/locations/1506/**
Fall City Historical Society: **http://www.fallcityhis-torical.org/**
Fall City historic signs walking tour map: **http://www.fallcityhistorical.org/downloads/signs/walk-ing-tour-brochure.pdf**
History walking tour itinerary: **http://savorsnoqualmieval-ley.org/itinerary/fall-city-historic-walking-tour/**

Designed as a public artwork at the Cedar River Watershed Center, these drums play to the rhythm of the rain or computer-generated droplets.

NORTH BEND

A MOUNTAIN LAKE, A LOST TOWN & RAIN DRUMS

A route along the lake provides haunting glimpses of history and artistic views of nature.

LENGTH: About 1.5 miles

DIFFICULTY RATING: Easy

SURFACES: Paved and gravel paths

STARTING POINT: North entrance to the Cedar River Watershed Education Center, 17905 Cedar Falls Rd. SE, North Bend, WA 98045

PARKING: Parking lots at north and south ends of the Education Center complex

PUBLIC TRANSIT: None nearby

KIDS WILL ENJOY: The sandy beach area at Rattlesnake Lake Park, the rain drums and activity days at the Education Center, and imagining life in the days of a now-lost town.

SERVICES ALONG ROUTE OR NEARBY: Restrooms at Education Center and beach area. Restaurants, gas, and retail in North Bend.

Route Description

Important Note: Access to the Education Center complex is on a road with a gate that is locked when the facility is closed. Check the posted closing time and keep an eye on the clock to make sure you remove your car before the gate is locked. As an alternative, park at Rattlesnake Lake and do this walk in reverse, although you will only be able to access the Education Center during the facility's open hours.

CEDAR RIVER WATERSHED EDUCATION CENTER Start at the entrance to the Education Center complex from the north parking lot. The map kiosk here will orient you to the area.

Walk on the covered walkway to the rain drum area, an audio and visual piece of public art. Restrooms located here; notice the planted roofs on top of these buildings.

You may want to go inside the visitor center building now or at the end of the walk. Stop in the library building if open to view the extensive displays about history of the watershed, its communities of workers and their families, and the flood that now covers a town with Rattlesnake Lake. As you walk through this complex, explore the side paths for peek-a-boo views of the lake.

At the south end of the buildings, walk past the fire circle area, then turn left to the junction with the gravel path. Read the history sign about the railroad houses and buildings that were once on the spot. Follow the gravel path to the south parking lot. Walk onto the concrete foundation for the railroad power substation and read the history sign about its operation. Step onto the paved pathway to the west of the foundation and walk south, following the path as it curves right/west toward the lake. You will likely hear, but may not be able to see, a stream as it enters the lake.

Continue walking and as you start to see the lake, low water levels may give you a view of old tree stumps and old pilings that indicate the town site of Moncton, which was suddenly and unexpectedly flooded in 1915 after construction of a water storage dam upstream in the watershed. Small dirt side paths provide lake access.

Continue walking north on the main path, looking for signs about the local history and natural features. Also notice the abundance of native trees and shrubs on both sides as well as benches with views of the lake and Rattlesnake Ledge to the west. Portable toilets are located along the path.

When you reach a small bridge, pause to enjoy the sight, sound, and refreshingly cool air of a rushing stream as it heads to the lake. Continue north on the main path until you reach the beach area for Rattlesnake Lake, reading the signs that high-light local wildlife.

To return to the Education Center, retrace your route along the main paved pathway. As an alternative, when you reach the junction with a gravel trail on your left, follow that path for a slightly shorter but slightly more uphill route to reach the Education Center north parking lot.

Inside the visitor center building, take time to view the exhibits, history photos and objects; shop for nature books and gifts; and talk to the ranger about upcoming tours and educational programs. Two pieces of public art are installed here: the tree roots design embedded in the concrete floor and the roots with neon lights hanging from the ceiling.

Before you return to your car, take a moment to enjoy one last view of the lake and remember the early loggers, railroad workers, and families who made a life here.

Exploration Ideas

- *Can you imagine what it would have been like to live and work here in the early 20th century?*
- *What did you learn about local plants and animals on this walk? Did you learn why this lake is named Rattlesnake?*
- *Why do you think the artist chose to bring tree roots inside the building? Can you predict which rain drum will play next?*

Nearby Walks and Points of Interest

Snoqualmie Valley Historical Museum in North Bend: **https:// www.snoqualmievalleymuseum.org/**

The historic train depot at 205 McClellan Street in North Bend is open seasonally for rides on vintage trains: **https:// trainmuseum.org/**

The Savor Snoqualmie Valley website offers a history walking itinerary for downtown North Bend: **https://savorsnoqualmi-evalley.org/itinerary/north-bend-historic-walking-tour/**

Meadowbrook Farm Park offers walking trails and a public art installation that honors Marie Louis, a Snoqualmie medicine woman: **https://www.meadowbrookfarmpreserve.org/ marie-louie-project.html**

Several hiking trails are located in the Rattlesnake Lake area; best for experienced and equipped hikers.

Check for Updated Information

Cedar River Watershed Education Center: **www.seattle. gov/util/crwec**

The Northwest Railway Museum in Snoqualmie is housed in the oldest train depot continuously operating in Washington

SNOQUALMIE

EXPLORATIONS BEYOND THE FALLS

A loop walk through the historic downtown and residential areas offers views of trains, the river, artworks, and logging history.

LENGTH: About 1.5 miles

DIFFICULTY RATING: Easy

SURFACES: Sidewalks (some rough and narrow), a few gravel roadsides

STARTING POINT: Northwest Railway Museum (train depot), 38625 SE King St., Snoqualmie, WA 98065

PARKING: Street parking along Railroad Ave. SE, in a parking lot north of the depot, and on side streets

PUBLIC TRANSIT: Snoqualmie Valley Transit

KIDS WILL ENJOY: Imagining travel on the vintage trains; playground at Riverview Park

SERVICES ALONG ROUTE OR NEARBY: Restrooms at train depot and Riverview Park. Restaurants, gas, and retail in downtown Snoqualmie.

Route Description

SNOQUALMIE TRAIN DEPOT This walk begins at the north end of the train depot, the oldest one still operating in Washington state. The depot is also part of the Northwest Railway Museum. Read the information sign about the depot's history and architecture style. Explore the displays within the depot and imagine travel as a passenger in the restored waiting room. If the depot isn't open, you can still view the vintage railcars and other items on display outside. Restrooms located at the south end of the depot.

RAILROAD AVE. SE TO SE RIVER ST. Return to the north end of the depot to cross the tracks, then turn right/south to walk on the west sidewalk along Railroad Ave. Read the information signs that indicate the landmark trees; notice the deep lines and patterns in the bark of these old trees. Also view the painted totem pole; a sign tells the story of the symbols. At the northwest corner of Railroad Ave. SE and SE River St., look at the large wheel saved from a nearby historic sawmill.

Cross Railroad Ave. SE and look at the two carved stone columns and the river design embedded in the concrete on the northeast corner of the intersection.

Cross SE River St. and notice the vintage steam clock and the train wheel design carved into the crosswalk.

A great town for railroad enthusiasts, Snoqualmie offers a rich sense of history throughout the downtown area.

SE RIVER ST. TO FALLS AVE. SE Walk east on SE River St. for one block, then cross and turn right on Falls Ave. SE, noticing the painted train wheels in the crosswalk and the historic brick bank building and hardware store/mercantile at this intersection. Walk south along the east side of Falls Ave. SE, enjoying the atmosphere of vintage homes and gardens.

FALLS AVE. SE TO PARK AVE. SE/RIVERVIEW PARK Turn left on SE Newton St. and walk one block to Riverview Park on the east side of Park Ave. SE. Restrooms, a playground, and picnic area located here; the Snoqualmie River is visible through a fence, although there is no access to the river bank.

PARK AVE. SE TO SE RIVER ST. Exit the park and cross to the west side of Park Ave. SE, then turn right/north. Notice how many of the houses have raised foundations to keep the living areas from being flooded when the river levels rise in the fall and winter. At the corner of SE River St., look at the unfenced view of the river and, if the weather permits, look behind you to a view of Mount Si to the southeast.

SE RIVER ST. TO RAILROAD AVE. SE TO SILVA AVE. SE Turn left/west on SE River St. and walk two blocks to cross Railroad Ave. SE and continue walking west. More vintage homes and gardens are visible as you walk through this neighborhood. Take a moment to reflect on the military memorial next to the American Legion building.

SILVA AVE. SE TO SE FIR ST. At Silva Ave. SE, turn right/north. At the northwest corner of SE King St. and Silva Ave. SE is the former Snoqualmie Valley High School building, a registered historical site.

SE FIR ST. TO RAILROAD PARK Continue walking north to reach Fir St., then turn right/east and cross Maple Ave. Walk to the park area at Railroad Pl. SE, then turn right/south and follow the paved path. Look for the old mill wheel and logging machinery display and read the information sign. Follow the path toward the Snoqualmie Depot; picnic tables located near the gazebo.

An old-fashioned gazebo in Snoqualmie makes a great photo stop.

RAILROAD PARK TO SE KING ST. Exit the park at the south end and cross the railroad tracks to the northwest corner of Railroad Ave. SE and SE King St. to view a three-part stone sculpture with a variety of elements reflecting local nature. Be sure to look at all sides of each piece to see everything.

Cross SE King St. for return to the depot.

Exploration Ideas

- What activities would you have seen at the depot when it was actively used for transporting people and freight?

- Along Railroad Ave., which symbols do you see in the totem pole and how many landmark trees can you count? Did you see the mural of logging trucks? (Hint: Look on the east side of the street, next to the parking lot for a strip mall.)

- Look for the giant log in Railroad Park; can you imagine how big that tree might have been?

- At the three-part stone sculpture, how many different nature elements did you see?

Nearby Walks and Points of Interest

A train ride from the Snoqualmie Depot will give you more insight into the community and local history. Also consider visiting the nearby Railroad History Center for a close-up look at the museum's work to restore vintage train cars.

An in-depth guide for a history-focused walking tour of downtown Snoqualmie is available at: **http://savorsnoqualmievalley.org/itinerary/snoqualmie-historic-walking-tour/details/**

Snoqualmie Falls Park, located at 6501 Railroad Ave. SE, is the area around the impressive local landmark, Snoqualmie Falls. You can reach the park by walking north on the paved pathway along Railroad Ave. SE and through the Salish Lodge parking area; approximately 2.5 miles round-trip. Find the route on the City of Snoqualmie trails map: **https://www.ci.snoqualmie.wa.us**

Most people find it easier to drive to the Falls parking area on the east side of Highway 203, then use the pedestrian bridge to access the walking trails and viewpoints within the park. History information signs are posted inside the pedestrian bridge; restrooms and picnic tables in the park.

Just south of the Salish Lodge, look for signs at the road to the Snoqualmie Falls Hydroelectric Museum (open seasonally). Informative exhibits are housed in the historic carpenter shop and train depot and show the impressive engineering behind the power plant. You'll also see what life was like for workers and their families at the turn of the 20th century.

Snoqualmie Valley History Museum in North Bend presents exhibits about local history, including the early communities of Snoqualmie and nearby Meadowbrook.

Check for Updated Information

City of Snoqualmie: **https://www.ci.snoqualmie.wa.us/**

Northwest Railway Museum (Snoqualmie Depot and Railroad History Center): **https://www.trainmuseum.org/**

Snoqualmie Falls Park: **http://www.snoqualmiefalls.com/**

Snoqualmie Falls Hydroelectric Museum: **https://www.pse.com/pages/tours-and-recreation/snoqualmie-tours**

Snoqualmie Valley History Museum: **www.snoqualmievalleymuseum.org**

IDEAS FOR MORE EXPLORATION

I hope the walks in this book have sparked a new level of curiosity about all the wonderful places to explore on Seattle's Eastside. The tips below can help you find new discoveries.

CITY PARKS DEPARTMENTS. Many city governments on the Eastside offer guided nature walks and park events.

ART EXHIBITS IN PUBLIC BUILDINGS. City Hall or community center galleries are maintained by Bothell, Kenmore, Mercer Island, and Sammamish; other communities may have occasional exhibits. Attend exhibit openings and artist receptions or go to the gallery during open hours to view the current exhibit.

LOCAL HISTORY EVENTS. Check with local historical societies for open hours, history walks, kid-friendly programs, tours, and other exploration activities.

ART IN AND AROUND THE LIBRARY. All King County libraries have interior artworks and many have artworks on the outside as well. Ask the librarian for information on art at that location and check out the book Art in Libraries, which highlights art across the entire library system.

LOOK FOR BOX WRAPS. Many Eastside cities have programs to wrap metal utility and traffic signal boxes with images from local artists or historical photos. Finding and tracking all the covered boxes in your community or while on one of these walks can make a fun exploration activity, especially with kids.

You can find out about many of these activities on the websites for cities and organizations, and by signing up for their email alerts.

And be sure to check out the updated resources for this book:

Website: **www.eastsideseattlewalks.com**
Facebook: Eastside Seattle Walks
Instagram: eastsideseattlewalks
Twitter: EastsideSeattleWalks
Pinterest: eastsideseattlewalks

PS: Have you found this book useful? Does it inspire you to walk more? I'd be grateful if you would spread the word:

→ Post a review on the book's Amazon page.
→ Share the book information on your Facebook, Instagram, or Twitter account.
→ Include the hashtag #eastsideseattlewalks in posts about your walking explorations!

Eastside Seattle Walks Author Janice King

ABOUT THE AUTHOR

JANICE KING is a writer, fiber artist, walking tour leader, and longtime Eastside Seattle resident. She believes in the value of walking for exploration and discovery, developing a sense of place, and deepening connection to community.

Janice is available to community groups as a speaker on Eastside walking attractions and walking as a community development and artistic practice. For topics and contact information visit: **www.eastsideseattlewalks.com/events**

INDEX